On the Other Side of the Garden

Living Biblical Womanhood in Today's World

By
Virginia Fugate

Aletheia Division of Alpha Omega Publications
Tempe, Arizona

All Scripture quotations are taken from the
New Scofield Reference Bible, Authorized King James Version

On the Other Side of the Garden
Copyright © 1992 by Virginia Fugate

Published by Aletheia Division of Alpha Omega Publications,

Credits
Sections I and II edited by Vera Allen
Section III edited by Tim Peelen
Cover Art by Mark Dinsmore
Inside illustrations by Melisa Evers Corwin & Tye Rausch

Printed in the United States of America

ISBN 0-86717-008-5

DEDICATION

to the glory of God

ACKNOWLEDGEMENTS

How can I give the proper credit to all those who influenced the writing of this book? There have been so many, I am sure to miss someone. I will never forget those who were instrumental in leading me to where I could hear the Gospel of Christ. They surrounded me in 1968 with their witness and their testimonial lives.

There was Dr. Lowell Wendt, my first pastor, who in 1968 made my need for salvation known. Under his teaching I accepted Christ and he led my oldest daughter to Christ. He baptized me, my husband, and two of my three children over a two-year period.

There was Vickie Kraft who in 1970 was an instructor for Child Evangelism Fellowship. At that time I was completely ignorant about the Word of God. I joined CEF thinking I wanted to teach children, and I ended up the one being taught. I sat mesmerized as God taught me, through Vickie, that His love, grace, and provision could be real in my life. I was thirty years old, but I was as a child learning His Word.

There were the excellent Bible teachers, including my own husband, under whom I studied for many years. I owe them so much. Through their teachings I learned the Word of God and began to realize His will for my life.

Last, but not least, were those who read the rough draft of this book and gave their excellent suggestions, constructive criticisms, advice, and encouragement. I am particularly grateful to Vera Allen and Tim Peelen both of whom edited the book extensively. I thank God for bringing Vera and Tim into my life and for using them now to compensate for my writing deficiencies. Of course, I take the full credit for any errors that remain.

I am grateful to all these dedicated believers. Much of this book is a result of their teachings, help, and encouragement. My deepest gratitude, however, is to God and for all that He has created. He was faithful even when I failed, and when His Word was the focus of my life it always proved victorious. To Him there can be no repayment; I can offer only my reverence and devotion. My earnest prayer is that this book will honorably represent my Lord Jesus Christ and the God of all creation.

Virginia Fugate

TABLE OF CONTENTS

SECTION I. FOUNDATIONS

SECTION II. OPPOSITIONS TO
BIBLICAL WOMANHOOD

SECTION III.　APPLICATIONS FOR
PRACTICAL LIVING

FOREWORD

This book was written for your benefit and to the glory of God. There has been no attempt to manipulate your emotions or to appeal to your vanity in its message. Only the woman who desires to know the truth and to serve God is likely to complete the book at all. It is a straight forward, no apologies, presentation of biblical truths about God's design for the woman and for the most important human relationship of her life—marriage.

After fifteen years of collecting notes on womanhood, my precious wife has overcome her fears and put her studies in writing. She has read book after book, hoping someone else had already done what she believed was needed, but to no avail. More and more, she has found that Christian books on marriage reflect a psychological approach to the husband/wife relationship. In other words, they promote people-managing techniques on how to get others to do what you want. Some of these techniques are just good ole' common sense like, "You can catch more flies with honey than you can with vinegar." Others are unabashed recommendations on how to manipulate your husband to achieve your goals. Understanding where your husband is psychologically, and how to better communicate to him, is a valuable asset for interpersonal relationships. However, this approach doesn't deal with who you are, what you should be doing, and what God's desire is in the issue.

The following scenario, taken from a child training example, shows the difference between the psychological approach and the biblical approach. A petite, four-year-old, pig-tailed girl was playing with her dolls in the park when another little girl walked by with her doll in a baby stroller. Little Miss Petite had an immediate attack of covetousness and wanted to stroll her dollies too. She pushed the other girl away from the stroller, threw out her baby, and started off with her own dollies warmly wrapped up.

Fortunately, little Miss Petite's mother observed the whole event from a nearby park bench. She arrived on the scene, stopped her darling little one, and began to give her instructions for living.

Psychological Approach

The mother descends on her little girl, returns the stroller to the other crying girl, and takes her daughter aside for a good talking to. Mother carefully explains to her child that she will make enemies and experience hurt if she treats people like she just treated the little girl with the stroller. Mother also suggests better ways to deal with the situation.

1) The daughter should go and meet the little girl and perhaps share her own dollies for a while. Then she might be able to borrow the girl's stroller.

2) Or, maybe the daughter could offer the little girl a piece of candy, or something else, for the use of the stroller.

Notice that the focus of this approach is on what the daughter might **lose** as a result of her behavior plus what she might **gain** by using different techniques.

Biblical Approach

The mother catches her daughter and makes her return the stroller and apologize to the other little girl (teaching the acceptance of personal accountability). She then takes her daughter aside to explain that she was wrong for pushing the little girl and stealing her stroller. This rebuke exposes her daughter's sin nature traits of covetousness and self-centeredness as being unacceptable.

Next, the mother teaches her daughter what is expected of her by God and that she must obey God—even if she doesn't get what she thinks she wants at the moment. She is taught, *"Let nothing be done through strife or vainglory, but in lowliness of mind let each esteem others better than themselves"* *(Philippians 2:3).* And, *". . . Thou shalt love thy neighbor as thyself"* (and, therefore, not covet or steal, *Romans 13:9).* Notice that this approach deals directly with the person who has the problem, not the ones with whom he or she has a problem.

The biblical approach is exactly what is unique about **On the Other Side of the Garden**. It deals with who you, as a woman, really are. Like the daughter in the illustration, you will learn God's truth, which will enable you to be successful in your own personal spiritual growth. This book defines your special design within the plan of God and even lays out the purpose of your life from God's point of view. It is not just another book on husband-management designed to help you get the most out of your marriage. The information presented will, at times, seem very one sided because it doesn't deal with what your husband should be or do. Instead, this book is for you only and will allow you to live your life to the glory of God, even if your husband never does what he should with his own life.

Not only has my wife studied and taught biblical womanhood, she is a qualified "older woman" with the responsibility and the credentials to teach the younger women. In our thirty-four years of marriage, she has faithfully lived up to all the truths presented here, as she came to know each of them. She patiently lived as my helpmate for over twenty difficult years while I searched for my manhood. I know of no other woman whom I could better testify, "Ginny is truly a biblical woman who is living successfully in today's world." My prayer for each reader is that you might experience the relationship my wife and I now possess, which is largely due to her having lived most of her life according to the principles set forth in this book.

J. Richard Fugate

INTRODUCTION

The Christian woman today faces a more difficult task living her life according to biblical teachings than at any other time in history. She is surrounded by magazines, TV programs, billboards, textbooks, movies, and newspapers which contain information that in one way or another debases the biblical role of the woman. These influences are so dominant that even the Christian woman often forms her attitudes and opinions from human sources, rather than basing them on God's Word. Without the knowledge of God's Word, she has nothing but the opinions of others and her own feelings to guide her.

There is a wide variance in the level of understanding and commitment to biblical womanhood among Christian women today. This variance is proof that antibiblical sources of information have successfully influenced, and confused, many Christian women. Although some women truly attempt to live their lives in accordance to God's will, a considerably larger number have been influenced into a life of combining Christian standards with whatever is popular opinion. Such women live suspended awkwardly between biblical womanhood and conformity with the world. Other Christian women have abandoned the biblical model entirely and have so conformed themselves to the world that they are indistinguishable from it.

On the Other Side of the Garden was written from a biblical perspective and is meant to offset the predominantly one-sided information that women see and hear about womanhood today. The purpose of this book is to provide biblical insight to all Christian women about the importance of biblical womanhood. It is my hope that God will use what I have written to foster a renewed commitment to the Word of God and to encourage Christian women to live their lives as testimonies to the correctness of God's design for biblical womanhood.

On the Other Side of the Garden is divided into three distinct sections:

Section I, *Foundations*, is the establishment of the principles of biblical womanhood from God's perspective. God created the woman and "designed" her for a specific purpose. The terms, "God's design for womanhood," or "womanhood's design," used extensively throughout this book, refer to more than just the woman's role as wife, mother, and homemaker. They refer to the purpose of God for the woman in every area of her life including her uniqueness, her importance, and her responsibilities. *Foundations* forms the premise on which the next two sections are based.

Section II, *Oppositions to Biblical Womanhood*, alerts Christian women to the antibiblical position of today's consistent attack against biblical womanhood. Satan's subtle deceptions are so masterful that women who desire autonomy have been easy prey for his conquest. This section will help to identify the lies that lead women away from biblical womanhood.

Section III, *Applications For Practical Living*, expounds on the biblical foundations presented in Section I and applies them to real life. I have personally practiced these principles in my own life, or have observed them in the lives of those close to me. I have made many of the mistakes that I am now warning you about. I have fallen into pits of despair that you could easily avoid, and I have learned some of what I know the hard way. Although experience may be the best teacher, it is also the most harsh teacher in terms of heartache and stress. Learning the material in this section could help you avoid some of those heartaches. It could also help you climb out of your own pits of despair and correct errors in which you are already involved. The practical applications will lead you to where you can receive the blessings that God promises to those who live according to His design, to those who apply the principles of biblical womanhood to their daily lives.

My Prayer

My fervent prayer is for each woman who reads this book. May she be refreshed, encouraged, and stimulated to a renewed eagerness for God's truths. The results of her hearing and obeying God will be a heightened sense of self-worth, a reinvigorated marriage, and a strengthened family. For these things may she give honor and praise to God alone. I pray further that her life will present to the world a praiseworthy example of God's design for womanhood. This prayer is offered in Jesus' name and for His glory.

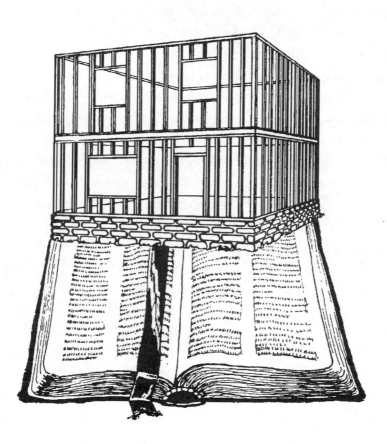

SECTION I

FOUNDATIONS

CHAPTER I

WHATEVER HAPPENED TO OLD-FASHIONED LOVE?

A popular song begins with, "Whatever happened to old-fashioned love?" The singer yearns for a love that would see him through the good times and the bad times; the kind of love that would last into his old age, a love like his grandparents had. Every time I hear that song, my heart goes out to all those husbands and wives who are missing an "old-fashioned love" in their marriages.

Why does old-fashioned love seem to be missing from our society today? Unfortunately, it is because most couples expect the immature, emotional attraction they first felt for one another to carry their marriage forever. In reality, however, they soon find that the "magic" is gone, and what is left are problems and children. Modern men and women are frequently unaware that a good marriage, like any other worthwhile endeavor in life, requires knowledge and hard work. They don't know that what our grandparent's generation really had was the character to stick it out through thick and thin.

What has happened to old-fashioned love? People have thrown it away or traded it for something new and valueless. They have given up on developing the oneness of marriage and have replaced it with the singleness of self-interest. They have discarded commitment and made instant self-gratification the criteria for determining life's choices. Demanding autonomy, they put self first above all others, and they claim the right to "do it my way." They are looking for fulfillment, but they will not find it; they might as well be looking for an ice cube on the sun.

How does a married couple develop old-fashioned love? It is the result of a strong attachment to each other long after the physical/emotional attraction wanes. The attraction stage of love that draws a man and woman to one another can happen in an instant, as in "love at first sight." But the attachment stage of love must be developed over a long period of time. There is no substitute for the companionship between two people who have years of memories in common: the same people, places, music, and events. A couple who has raised children together (and survived to tell about it) have memories that continue long after the children are grown. Warm memories, such as how we laughed when the baby said she had "pilty peet" while playing in the mud, continue to unite us as we use this phrase ourselves when gardening. In the attachment stage of love the couple is so united that each member knows without a word being spoken what the other is feeling, thinking, wanting, or needing. They can even finish each other's sentences.

Nothing bonds a couple like living through illnesses and family crises. And there is no love like the love that has been tested to its very limits, and has grown stronger. Love becomes more meaningful for those who live through

2

heartbreaks that seem as if they will never mend, yet somehow always do. The reward for those who work at developing the attachment stage is a strengthened love that is worth any pain or effort to acquire.

After all the years of overcoming trials together, it is wonderful to find that you still thrill when he smiles at you from across a room. And that he still tells you he loves you. It is delightful to kiss the bald spot on top of his head and for him to see past your "laugh lines." It is comforting to grow older together, and to continue to love.

Peace reigns when all the battles have been won and the questions have been answered about who and where each one gives or takes. The best of times begin only after the self-centered motivations of youth are replaced with other-centered love, respect, and the fulfillment of mutual giving and caring. It is comforting to find that, together, you flow like a two-person canoe on a gentle stream, both paddling in the same direction; to know that if you hit rapids, the experience of rowing as one will continue and carry you to safety. Now, you each have a friend who provides a safe haven on earth and a life-sustaining security.

Can a Christian woman live a biblical life and experience old-fashioned love in this modern world? Not only can she, but the people she loves are depending on her to do just that. Her husband needs her as a biblical wife and her children, as well as future generations, learn from her example.

That ye may be blameless and harmless, children of God, without rebuke, in the midst of a crooked and perverse nation, among whom ye shine as lights in the world. Holding forth the word of life . . .   *Philippians 2:15-16a*

Our nation desperately needs Christian women who trust God's Word enough actually to live by its precepts. We need women who will live as testimonies to God's truths.

As you read this book you will probably experience several different emotional reactions. At times you will be filled with inspiration over the purity of God's Word, and at other times you will agonize over the difficulty of your everyday reality. But, just as there is joy within the attachment stage of human love, there is also immeasurable joy from, *"holding forth the word of life."* I pray that God will use this book to raise you above the pressures of today and enter you into the enduring satisfaction that is offered only by a lifetime of biblical womanhood.

CHAPTER II

CREATION WITH A PURPOSE

"Who am I? Why am I here?" Every intelligent woman will consider these questions at some point in her life. She realizes that without the correct answers her life could be spent in vain. This is especially true for the Christian woman who desires to live a godly life. Can a woman know her true identity? Can she actually possess complete confidence that she is living her life for a worthwhile purpose? Yes, she can! This chapter establishes the principles upon which biblical womanhood is founded. Knowledge of this biblical foundation allows a woman to comprehend her true design and purpose in life. When she then functions according to God's design, she is able to have fulfillment in her marriage, success in the training of her children, and confidence in her relationships with others.

What source provides more accurate information about the design and purpose of a creation than the manual written by the original designer? The Bible is just such a manual. Understanding God's master plan is necessary in order to answer a woman's questions about life. To answer the question, "Who am I?", it is first essential to understand God's pattern, or original blueprint, of the woman. To answer the question, "Why am I here?", we must discover God's purpose in His design for the woman. With complete accuracy, the Bible tells us why the woman was created, and it defines her purpose and function within God's plan as a part of His creation. The first section of this book is dedicated to revealing this biblical blueprint and God's designed purpose for the woman.

God's Purposes for the Creation of Mankind

Originally, mankind was complete and perfect, as was all of God's creation. God had a specific purpose for each part of His creation that went beyond its mere existence. For instance, one of His purposes for mankind was to have productive work, as demonstrated in *Genesis 2:15, "And the Lord God took the man, and put him into the garden of Eden to till it and to keep it."*

God did not leave man without clear instructions as to what He expected of Him. He communicated with Adam, because He intended that mankind should know and obey His Word. He established His authority over mankind with precise instructions that carried specific consequences for disobedience. Adam was told that he might freely eat of every tree in the garden, *"But of the tree of the knowledge of good and evil, thou shalt not eat of it; for in the day that thou eatest thereof thou shalt surely die" (Genesis 2:17).*

Awareness of Being Incomplete

Adam had all he needed and was unaware of any incompleteness or loneliness until God brought it to his attention. God, not Adam, said, *". . . It is not good that the man should be alone; I will make him an help fit for him"* (Genesis 2:18). God used a parade of creatures to prepare Adam for the presentation of a helper appropriate for him.

> *And out of the ground the Lord God formed every beast of the field, and every foul of the air; and brought them unto Adam to see what he would call them . . .*
> Genesis 2:19a

Apparently, both male and female creatures were brought before Adam, because it was during this parade of tangible evidence that Adam noticed he was alone.

> *And Adam gave names to all cattle, and to the fowl of the air, and to every beast of the field; but for Adam there was not found an help fit for him.*
> Genesis 2:20

Separation of the Woman

The woman as a separate entity was not created at the same time, or in the same way, as was the original creation of mankind.

> *And the rib, which the Lord God had taken from the man, made he a woman, and brought her unto the man.*
> Genesis 2:22

When God created the woman, He did not manufacture her from the raw materials of the earth as He did the original body of mankind. Instead, God took the essence of the woman directly out of His first creation of mankind. This does not mean that woman was an afterthought of God, for her essence was created from the beginning as an integral part of the species called mankind.

> *So God created man in His own image, in the image of God created he him; male and female created he them.*   *Genesis 1:27*

Biblical studies in the original Hebrew language of Genesis have determined that the original human creation consisted of one body containing both the masculine and the feminine characteristics of mankind.[1] These studies indicate that just as the physical material (the rib) was removed from the original human creation and used to construct the first woman's body, the woman's immaterial essence (her soul) was also removed from the original human creation and used to animate her newly formed body.

We are certain that the creation of the woman was not at all like that of the original human. The first human was physically formed out of the dust of the ground, but the woman was physically fashioned out of that first human's rib. Also, God breathed life into the first human and soul life came into existence. Nothing, however, is said about God breathing life into the woman. Could this be because her soul was already animated and entwined with that of the man's?

God simply molded a second human body around Adam's rib. He then placed the female soul, which He apparently also removed from the original creation, into that second body. In this way, the separation of the female from the original creation of mankind resulted in two distinct entities—man and woman. This division removed from Adam most of the feminine characteristics, leaving him predominately masculine. Conversely, the newly formed woman possessed mostly feminine characteristics. Mankind was no longer the whole, complete creation that it was in the beginning. Two separate entities now existed, each needing the other to make mankind whole again.

This helps to explain the mystery of marriage, the rejoining of the two back into one flesh. The term flesh is often used scripturally for man's immaterial, as well as for his material, essence. Marriage is a rejoining of the two parts into one, like original creation. We know from observing life that there is a partial soul-uniting between normal (unscarred by promiscuity) men and women as they begin to have physical contact. After physical intercourse, their souls are even more intertwined, especially the woman's. Any separation then cannot be done without soul damage to both; it is as if that which had become one is ripped apart.

And (God) *said, For this cause shall a man leave father and mother, and shall cleave to his wife, and they two shall be one flesh. Wherefore, they are no more two, but one flesh. What, therefore, God hath joined together, let no man put asunder.*
Matthew 19:5-6

This important message is also recorded in *Genesis 2:24* and repeated in *Ephesians 5:31*.

The Returned Rib

God's purpose in forming the woman was to provide for Adam a mate corresponding to himself. God had taken from Adam all that was necessary to form both the material and the immaterial parts, the body and soul, of a separate being. He then returned to Adam all of these parts in the form of the woman—a counterpart to the man.

Adam was not unaware of the origin of the woman. His first response to seeing her indicates his recognition of her source.

> *And Adam said, This is now bone of my bones, and*
> *flesh of my flesh; . . .*   *Genesis 2:23a*

Adam had named the creatures of earth, so it was natural for him to give a name to the woman—one that would match her purpose for being. Original creation had one generic name, Adam or mankind, but now there were two bodies and two names. Man was now distinctly male, and woman was distinctly female. The Hebrew word for "man" is *Ish*, and the Hebrew word for "woman" is *Isha* (meaning "out of Ish").

> *And Adam said, . . . she shall be called Woman,*
> (Isha), *because she was taken out of Man.* (Ish).
>   *Genesis 2:23*

12

God's Purpose for Woman

Even before the female essence was brought forth out of Adam, the woman's purpose was stated by God. He had said that it was not good for man to be alone. The man needed a companion and a helper suitable for him. That companion and helper was a component of himself placed in a separate body and named woman. The naming of "Isha" reveals Adam's recognition of the woman as a counterpart to himself, and it indicates that he understood her purpose in functioning as his helpmate.

That the woman was the second entity to appear does not make her second-best, merely incomplete. By forming the woman **from** Adam, and by bringing her **to** him, God stressed the woman's dependence on, fulfillment in, and relationship to her man.

> *For the man is not of the woman, but the woman of the man. Neither was the man created for the woman, but the woman for the man.*
>
> I Corinthians 11: 8-9

God designed the woman for the man's benefit *(Genesis 2:18-20)*, and out from him *(Genesis 2:22-23)*, and for him *(I Corinthians 11:8-9)*. Remember, all the uniquely feminine attributes comprise only one-half of human creation. There is no indication anywhere in scripture that the married woman was to have a purpose of her own, apart from her mate. (See Appendix, Women Alone)

What Does Helper Mean?

The scriptural definition of "helper" is not greatly different from a dictionary definition: "a person or thing that helps or gives assistance, support, etc." Synonyms for helper include "aide," "assistant," "supporter," "backer," "auxiliary." The verb "to help" is defined: "To contribute strength or means to; render assistance to; cooperate effectively with; aid, assist: as in, 'he helped with my work'." [2]

These definitions indicate that the woman, as helper, is an assistant—the one who helps to achieve the goals of the one leading. His goals become her goals. She cooperatively and effectively assists and renders aid, strengthening the man for his own tasks. A woman has important work to do. She should use her intelligence, talents, and abilities in such a way that her efforts give support and encouragement to her man. This could range from providing a stable, comfortable home to working in her husband's business or to giving moral support of his ministry. In other words, she helps her husband in whatever capacity he most needs her assistance.

Scripture never indicates that the woman is lacking in intelligence or abilities. In fact, in order for her to be able to accomplish her tasks, God provides certain excellent abilities that appear to be mainly feminine characteristics. Women tend to be compassionate, understanding, patient, tenacious, and unselfishly nurturing of others.

The woman obviously must have ability, or she would be of no help at all; she would merely be in the way. In fact, the woman who rejects her position as helper is in the way no matter what her abilities may be. Such a woman renounces her own purpose within God's creation. As a result she can even hinder her man's development and her family's growth toward God's desired objectives.

Some modern women reject God's design because they mistakenly believe that His purpose for them as helpers is lowly in importance. They confuse subordinance with inferiority and think that the subordinate position of helper is demeaning. Perhaps these women have never fully analyzed their thoughts in light of God's Word. How could any of God's intended purposes for His creation be demeaning? All that God created deserves exaltation, including His purpose for both man and woman. The woman who lives according to God's perfect design is not degraded; instead, she reflects the beauty of original creation and fulfills the purpose for which she was born. This is the woman who can confidently answer the questions, "Who am I? Why am I here?"

CHAPTER III

THE DECEPTION

The woman was designed by God to function in the supportive role of helpmate to her husband. It was God's plan that husband and wife operate as one, as a single harmonious creation. Nearly every woman desires, even longs for, such a oneness of soul with a man. Why, then, does it appear to be so difficult to achieve compatibility and oneness in marriage today? What has happened?

To answer these questions we must return to the time of the original creation. In the very beginning, Satan challenged God's right to rule over him.

> *For thou* (Satan) *hast said in thine heart, I will ascend into heaven, I will exalt my throne above the stars of God; . . . I will ascend above the heights of the clouds, I will be like the Most High.*
> *Isaiah 14:13-14*

This emphatic statement of rebellion was a rejection of God's rule, as well as Satan's declaration of war against God. Accordingly, everything he has done since this proclamation has been a perpetuation of this revolt. Satan's plot to entice mankind to join his rebellion against God began when he possessed the serpent and approached the woman in the Garden of Eden.

> *Now the serpent was more subtle than any beast of the field which the Lord God had made. And he said unto the woman, Yea, hath God said, Ye shall not eat of every* (false) *tree of the garden?*
>
> *Genesis 3:1*

Examine God's original instruction below and compare it to Satan's subtle alteration of God's words in the passage above, indicated by the emphases in both quotations. Observe how Satan asked a slanted question, distorting God's true command in order to make it seem unfair.

> *And the Lord God commanded the man, saying, Of every tree of the garden thou mayest freely eat; but of the tree of the knowledge of good and evil, thou shalt not eat of it; for in the day that thou eatest thereof thou shalt surely die.* (Emphasis added)
>
> *Genesis 2:16-17*

Satan led the way in the use of subtle alterations of God's Word in order to corrupt its meaning and deny its original purpose. The woman followed Satan's lead with her own seemingly minor modification of God's words.

> *And the woman said unto the serpent, We may eat of the fruit of the trees of the garden; but of the fruit of the tree which is in the midst of the garden, God hath said, Ye shall not eat of it,* (accurate so

18

far) *neither shall ye touch it,* (a little embellishment) *lest ye die.* (accurate again)

Genesis 3:2-3

By following his lead in modifying God's words, and by doubting God's intent and questioning His provision, the woman revealed herself to be ready to follow Satan's lead in rebelling against God's design and purpose for her. The stage now set, the serpent delivered his mortal thrust:

> *And the serpent said unto the woman, Ye shall not surely die; For God doth know that in the day ye eat thereof, then your eyes shall be opened, and ye shall be as God, knowing good and evil.*
>
> *Genesis 3:4-5*

(This is a lie! God had clearly communicated in *Genesis 2:17* that she **would** die.)

Satan claimed that God was deliberately withholding something of value from the woman. He implied that she was being deprived, and could obtain, without penalty, that which God withheld from her. He suggested that she was merely lacking that knowledge which would make her **like** God. Satan's intention was to lead the woman into disobedience by the same proud and rebellious route he himself had taken. In his evil rebellion, he had said, *"I will be like the Most High."* Notice the parallel in his offer of superior knowledge to the woman, *" . . . your eyes will be opened, and you will be like God" (Genesis 3:5b).* (Emphasis added)

19

Finally, convinced by Satan's smooth lies and distortions of God's Word, the woman took the fatal step toward rebellion against God—she acted in opposition to God's stated will.

> *And when the woman saw that the tree was good for food, and that it was pleasant to the eyes, and a tree to be desired to make one wise, she took of the fruit thereof, and did eat, and gave also unto her husband with her; and he did eat.*
>
> *Genesis 3:6*

By eating the fruit the woman was, in a sense, doing what was natural to her, following leadership. But she did not follow the leadership of the Lord, nor did she follow her husband. Instead, she followed the leadership of a seducer. The woman's fall into Satan's trap reveals her weakest and most vulnerable areas of temptation—an intense desire for knowledge and for self-rule. Additionally, a woman lacks discernment of Satan's deceptive tactics, and therefore is easily deceived. The easiest way to deceive a woman is to appeal to her lust for superior knowledge, or to tempt her with an offer of autonomy.

Although the woman was deceived, the man was not. The woman had such a powerful influence on the man that she was able to tempt him to choose, knowingly and willingly, to disobey God.

> *And Adam was not deceived, but the woman, being deceived, was in the transgression.*
>
> *I Timothy 2:14*

When the man followed the woman's lead, he revealed his weakest and most vulnerable area of temptation—the woman. The easiest way to tempt a man to fall away from God's will is by appealing to his desire for the woman. This desire is so strong that a man will even abandon his own principles to follow the wishes of a woman.

When the woman offered the fruit to the man, she stepped outside her designed role and purpose of helpmate. She acted, instead, as the leader. Similarly, when the man accepted the fruit from her hand, he rejected his designed purpose of headship and acted as a follower. These seemingly simple acts reversed the leadership and helpmate positions, violating the relative positions of leader and follower that God had intended to define the relationship between men and women. The "battle of the sexes," or, which-sex-will-lead-and-which-will-follow, was born.

The success of Satan's seduction of the woman and the willingness of the man to follow her into disobedience provided Satan with his most powerful weapon against the human race—knowledge of both the man's and the woman's weaknesses. To this day, he uses this knowledge to lure men and women into straying from God's plan and purpose for their lives.

Satan Still Deceives the Woman Today

Satan carried his personal war against God to the Garden of Eden, where he deceived the woman and used her to induce the man to rebel against God's created order. In the same way, with the same motives and techniques, Satan continues to wage his war against God through mankind. Satan still deceives women with half-truths and lies fabricated to promote unrest and dissatisfaction.

> *For of this sort are they who creep into houses, and lead captive silly women laden with sins, led away with various lusts, ever learning, and never able to come to the knowledge of the truth.*
> *II Timothy 3:6-7*

With the same insidious distortions that deceived Eve, Satan whispers to the modern woman:

Shed this ridiculous womanhood design, and you can be like God.

Women who hold to God's design for womanhood are old-fashioned, helpless, self-deprecating, and pathetic. God's design does not protect you; it actually harms you. It holds you back from personal development and denies you the right of self-expression.

You should be in control of your own life. Women are intelligent beings. You don't need a man to tell you what to do, especially if he is inferior in intelligence or maturity. Women can do anything as well as, or perhaps even better than, most men. In fact, a woman's solutions to problems are often much superior to a man's.

> Education about women's rights will give you
> the knowledge and backbone to fight for your
> freedom. Knowledge equals freedom, the
> freedom to be your own authority. (Perhaps...
> to be like God?)

Women today are assaulted from all sides with this barrage of flattering appeals that are aimed with great precision at their weakest points—their intense desire for knowledge and for autonomy. Enticements such as these continue to promote in women unrest and dissatisfaction with their created purpose. They encourage the woman to wrest from God His right to designate her design, and to take for herself total control over her own destiny. Those who promote these false teachings tell the woman that she will benefit by overthrowing male leadership. They imply that the woman who does not rebel against male leadership is ignorant, or that she is weak and has been bullied into submission. They deny that there are any negative consequences for pursuing a course of action which directly opposes God's will.

One vehicle through which Satan promotes his rebellion today is the women's liberation movement. The feminist movement appeals to the woman's desire for autonomy and promotes the reversal of God's intended order for mankind. This satanic philosophy has saturated the entertainment world with its almost universal portrayal of the independent woman—happy, fulfilled, and knowledgeable. She is shown to be successfully pursuing an important career, while just as successfully nurturing, and leading, a family—often compensating for the deficiencies of a weak man.

Camouflaging its contradictions with elegant language and just enough truth to make it plausible, Satan's false philosophy has infiltrated the news media with its cries of "sexism," while government at all levels has responded with laws for "women's rights."

Modern women are constantly bombarded with Satan's false philosophy. Women are exposed to feminist propaganda every day through television programs, newspaper reports, and magazine articles. Even those women who do not consciously embrace the rabidly radical positions of the women's liberation movement are, however, still affected by this continuous flow of propaganda. The constant repetition of the tenets of feminism causes such falsehoods to appear valid by their very familiarity. Evidence of this insidious influence is found even in the church, where fewer and fewer women are living their lives as biblical helpmates. Those young Christian women who **do** dare to put husband and family first are frequently made to feel inadequate and inferior, guilty of the "waste" of their unrealized potential.

In Conclusion

I believe the majority of women who are influenced by Satan's present-day deceptions are unaware that they are following his lead in rebelling against God's created order. The woman in the Garden of Eden would probably have recognized a more overt approach to lure her into disobedience to God. If Satan had picked the fruit and handed it to her, she might have recoiled. Instead, by appealing to her pride, he was able to trick her into disobeying God's command. Similarly, the modern woman's pride makes her vulnerable to the deceptive tactics of Satan. Because women have an insatiable thirst—to the point of lust—for wisdom and self-rule, they too often forsake God's original designed purpose for their lives and attempt to be their own authority. In acting autonomously, they believe themselves to be following no one's lead but their own. In actuality, they are supporters of Satan's rebellion, following his leadership, unwitting partners with him in his war against God.

CHAPTER IV

CURSING TURNED TO BLESSING

The first man and woman were blessed by living in the garden, but they were also warned that there would be consequences if they ate of the tree of the knowledge of good and evil. They did not take God's warning seriously and their disobedience is recorded in Genesis as mankind's first act of sin.

God judged Adam's and Eve's disobedience and sentenced them to specific penalties which they and all their unborn children would bear throughout time. In this chapter we will look at these penalties and at their repercussions on the modern woman. We will also discover how God provided ways to bless the biblical woman even though she must live with the consequences of mankind's original sin.

The Two Curses

When God judged the sin of the first woman, He pronounced a sentence that contained two penalties. The first penalty concerned her role in childbearing, and the second restated the already established pattern for her relationship with her husband.

Unto the woman He said, I will greatly multiply thy sorrow and thy conception; in sorrow thou shalt bring forth children; and thy desire shall be to thy husband, and he shall rule over thee.

Genesis 3:16

The first penalty that must be borne by women is the pain associated with the process of childbirth. Not only is childbirth painful, but a woman's whole reproductive system often causes her problems. The menstrual cycle is rarely less than bothersome, and for many women it is a severe monthly trauma. Even the cessation of the menstrual cycle (menopause) is difficult for many women. Pregnancy also includes trauma, from morning sickness and mood swings to backaches and unwanted weight gain. Finally, the process before delivery is aptly called "labor."

To focus only on the punishment side of this curse, however, is to forget that God's purpose for curses is to draw mankind to Himself. The Bible records at least seventy-seven times that God placed curses on mankind so that, *"thou mayest know that I am the Lord."* The pain in childbirth is not meant solely to punish, but also to teach. The pain and sorrow associated with childbirth is a reminder of the results of sin and the consequences of disobeying God.

The second penalty for the woman's sin is twofold: her desire for her husband, and the principle that a woman is to be ruled by her husband. Does this really mean what it appears to mean? Raymond C. Ortlund, Jr. in the book *Recovering Biblical Manhood & Womanhood*, has done

28

extensive research on the Hebrew word translated "desire" in *Genesis 3:16b*.[3] He has determined that the meaning of this word conveys a very strong urge for control. This same word is used in *Genesis 4:7b* where Cain is told that sin desires to control him, but instead, that he must rule over sin. *Genesis 3:16b* might be more easily understood as follows: You (woman) will "desire to control" your husband, but he will "rule" (have dominion, reign, have power) over you. A wife is cursed with being ruled by her husband while at the same time she has a strong urge to control him! The woman's "desire" is a weighty curse indeed. Her urge to control her husband may be as strong as the pull of sin was on Cain.

Because of the woman's desire to control, God's words "*. . . and he shall rule over thee*" bring gritting and gnashing of teeth to even naturally compliant women. No woman wants someone else to have power over her. She not only feels that she doesn't need anyone to rule over her, she also feels this strong desire to control her husband. Obviously, these drives are the source of the battle-of-the-sexes. While the husband's natural drive (and his responsibility) is to rule his wife, hers is to control him. Without God's grace there would be little hope for any marriage.

The Blessings

It is God's deepest desire to bless mankind (*I Timothy 2:3-4* and *John 3:17*). Therefore, whenever it is necessary for God's righteousness to judge for disobedience, His love provides a way to turn that cursing into blessing. Even though it may be hard for us to believe, the judgment on the woman's sin, which we might consider a "curse on womanhood," can be one of our greatest benefits. However, to obtain these benefits, it is necessary to understand God's provision for blessing within the penalty. Otherwise, the penalties remain cursing, while the benefits lay dormant and unclaimed.

Let's look at the first benefit contained within the judgment on the woman's sin. As we've seen, each childbirth was a painful reminder of the result of sin. But with the pain, God also provided the blessing of a new life. With each new life was an even more extraordinary blessing—the hope for the future birth of the promised Saviour *(Genesis 3:15b)*. Through this Saviour, the "seed" of the woman, all mankind is provided the way to a restored relationship with God.

> *Let this mind be in you, which was also in Christ Jesus, Who, being in the form of God, thought it not robbery to be equal with God, But made himself of no reputation, and took upon him the form of a servant, and was made in the likeness of men.* Philippians 2:5-7

Today, pain and sorrow in childbirth still continue to offer the blessing of a new life, and most women consider the pain of childbirth to be a small price to pay when they finally hold their newborn infant. Although women no longer look forward to the birth of the Saviour, we are now blessed with the reminder that He has already come. Through Him the curse of eternal separation from God has been overturned, and the blessing of eternal life is available to all those who "... *believe that Jesus is the Christ, the Son of God" (John 20:31b).*

The second benefit that God included within the penalty for the woman's sin concerns her need for protection from deception. God created women to be responders, companions, and helpmates to their own husbands. These characteristics make women excellent followers. However, because women are followers by nature, they will respond to, and follow, the allurements of evil deception, as occurred in *Genesis 3:1-5*. It was not only the first woman who fell for persuasive lies, however; modern woman is also susceptible to deception.

> *But I permit not a woman to teach, nor to usurp authority over the man, but to be in silence. For Adam was first formed, then Eve. And Adam was not deceived, but the woman, being deceived, was in the transgression.*
>
> I Timothy 2: 12-14

Deceived women are easily defrauded, beguiled, cheated, and misled. Through the centuries deceivers have misled women by appealing to their desire for autonomy, or to their lust for knowledge. Such beguiled women are then easily used to tempt their men to oppose God's will, just as Eve was used by Satan to tempt Adam. Because women are easily deceived, they need protection from those who would take advantage of this weakness. Therefore, God offers women protection by giving them leadership—through their husbands. In this manner, God has turned the cursing of subjection into the blessing of protection for those women who defer to their husband's leadership.

But, Men Are Sinners, Too!

It may be difficult at this point to understand how being subject to a man's authority can actually be beneficial to a woman. After all, the man sinned knowingly and deliberately, while the woman was simply misled. Any woman knows that men are subject to error, as well as to deliberate selfishness and sin. No man is always going to make good decisions, even with the best of intentions.

Therefore, a woman's first reaction to the command to submit to her husband's rule is often fear, anger, or even shock that God could possibly mean **that**! Her "desire" to control her husband and the realization that her earthly life, both present and future, are dependent on the decisions of another person frightens her. All kinds of "but what if's?" come to her mind. She can foresee that submitting to another's rule leaves her vulnerable, not only to error, but to intentional maltreatment as well. It is quite natural for a woman to fear that her man might take unfair advantage of his position of authority over her. It is also natural for her to attempt to maintain control over any decision that affects her. So then, how does a woman ever dare to trust in any man's leadership? Because, the biblical woman's protection is **not** dependent solely on the character of her husband; it is secured by the Character of God. When a woman submits to her husband, she is actually living out her trust in God.

> *For after this manner in the old time the holy women also, who trusted in God, adorned themselves, being in subjection unto their own husbands.*   *I Peter 3:5*

It is conceivable that a modern daughter of Eve may reject the idea that she needs protection from deception, even though God says that she does. But her disbelief does nothing to alter God's truth. Neither does her disbelief alter God's judgment on her disobedience. Any woman who rejects God's provision for her protection from deception and His gift of her husband's rule over her desire to control, constructs a barrier between herself and His plan. A woman who insists on being outside her husband's leadership places herself outside God's protection. In this vulnerable position, she is subject to the harmful effects of her own inherent weaknesses. Consequently, she is susceptible, not only to the deceptions of Satan, but also to the convincing arguments of all those who would seduce her away from the truth about her womanhood. In addition, she is totally subject to self-delusion created by her own pride and lust. When she persists in living outside God's plan, cursing remains cursing and cannot be overcome—even with all her human abilities.

The realization of the blessings and benefits incorporated within God's judgment on the sin of the woman is achieved only when a woman replaces her own desire for personal autonomy with a complete trust in God. When a woman obeys God by allowing her husband to lead, God Himself will stand as an impenetrable protective shield and protect her from herself and from outside deception. In this protected position, cursing is overcome and turned to blessing.

CHAPTER V

PRINCIPLES OF AUTHORITY

Authority! Here is a word that is bitterly despised by all rebels. An attitude of distrust and disrespect toward anyone in a position of leadership is prevalent today among even normally law-abiding people. Negative attitudes toward the concept of authority originate from man's misunderstandings about the proper meaning of, and purpose for, authority. These misunderstandings, added to personal experiences with leaders who have misused their power, have caused many people to fear and reject altogether the concept of authority.

Where there are positions of authority, logic dictates that there are also positions subordinate to those authorities. The concept of subjection is even more antagonistic to the human will than is the concept of authority—and therein lies man's true objection. It is much easier to accept one's own responsibility **as** the authority (such as a parent over children) than it is to accept personal subjection **to** one's own authority (such as a wife in submission to her husband). We will learn the important difference between submission and blind obedience in the next chapter.

Although this chapter is not actually about submission, it must be pointed out that objections to the concept of authority often stem from our own desire for autonomy. If you are already feeling irritated, you are not unusual. Most of us feel at least a twinge of resentment when confronted with the subject of authority. Remember, Eve wanted to be in control of her own life, and you are a daughter of Eve. While you read this chapter, try to set aside any objections to the concept of authority that have been caused by those people who have misused their authority. Instead, allow God to reveal how His authority system was designed to bless and protect you. Don't let Satan deceive you, as he deceived Eve, into rejecting the peace and security God has ordained for your benefit through His system of authority. Resentment of authority will only close your mind to God's will for your life.

We need to study the principles of authority so that we will not be deceived into an automatic reaction against the very system that God has established for our benefit. First, we will look at a generalized definition of authority. From that definition we will study some characteristics of God's supreme authority and then determine which principles apply to our subject—womanhood.

The General Definition of Authority

The definition of authority is: "the right to rule; the power to act, decide, command, and judge."[4] It is the right to set policy, the rulership position necessary to command subordinates, and the power to administer judgment to those who disobey and to reward those who conform.

At first glance, it might appear that authority is unbridled power that could easily be used to oppress those who are the subjects. It is true that there are, and always have been, those who abuse the power of authority. However, these abuses do not negate the fact that God has established a structure of authority. The power of authority is not without controls or limits. God has established rules and boundaries to govern the use of all authority. God is in the position and has the power to enforce His will over all other authorities and He never forfeits this control. His ultimate authority over all creation is the guarantee of protection to every person under authority.

God Is the Ultimate Authority

For the Lord Most High is awe-inspiring; he is a great King over all the earth.　　　*Psalm 47:2*

That men may know that thou, whose name alone is the Lord, art the Most High over all the earth.
　　　　　　　　　　　　　　　　Psalm 83:18

The word translated *"Most High"* is a title, and is used in Scripture for God only.[5] This title of *"Most High"* is never given to a member of the human race in his role as ruler. It is a title used only to describe God's position of absolute authority. He is the *Most High.* There is no other above Him with any right to rule.

. . . I blessed the Most High, and I praised and honored him who liveth forever, whose dominion

is an everlasting dominion, and His kingdom is
from generation to generation.
Daniel 4:34b

This passage recognizes the infinite extent of God's rule. There is no end to the reign of God. His timelessness establishes a sobering contrast to the insignificant period of time in which a human authority can exercise rulership. God is always in control!

God Has the Right to Dictate Our Roles in Life

But our God is in the heavens; he hath done
whatsoever he hath pleased.   *Psalm 115:3*

. . . Shall the thing formed say to him that formed
it, why hast thou made me thus? Hath not the
potter power over the clay, of the same lump to
make one vessel unto honor, and another unto
dishonor?   *Romans 9:20b-21*

God is the Creator. He has the right to rule His creatures according to His will and according to His design.

And all the inhabitants of the earth are reputed as
nothing; and he doeth according to his will in the
army of heaven, and among the inhabitants of the
earth, and none can stay his hand, or say unto him,
What doest thou?   *Daniel 4:35*

"And all the inhabitants of the earth are reputed as nothing" is a relative statement. It establishes a relationship between God's position of absolute authority (right to rule) and mankind's puny positions of authority. Nebuchadnezzar, the speaker in this verse, is king over a mighty kingdom, and he is saying that even as king he has no right to say to God, "What are you doing?" Notice that the sphere of God's rule include both the inhabitants of earth and the entire angelic creation, including Satan ("the army of heaven").

The conclusion that we can draw from these verses, and from many others on the subject, is that God as the Creator has the right to set the policy for all His creation according to His own will. He has the ultimate position of rulership above all the creatures whereby He may direct their actions. He also has the power to administer justice; in other words, He has the power to punish evil and to reward good. Since ultimate authority belongs to God, any legitimate right to rule must be delegated by Him.

No Authority Exists Except As Appointed by God

Let every soul be subject unto the higher powers.
For there is no power but of God: the powers that
be are ordained of God.   *Romans 13:1*

The Greek word translated "power" means "authority, the right to decide or act, ruling or official powers."[6]   God commands **every** individual to place himself willingly under the positions of human rulership that exist above him. How do we dare to do this? We can submit to our authorities because, as the verse then states, no ruling power exists unless sanctioned by God. Every position of human authority that He has established remains under His control. The word translated "ordained" means "to place, station, appoint or determine someone into an official position over others."[7] It is the Greek word from which the theological term "institution" is derived. The three basic institutions defined in Scripture which effect all humans are government, marriage, and family. God has instituted all existing positions of rulership that govern His creatures; God's purpose of all rulers is to carry out His will and to administer justice to those under their rule.

God's Word gives specific boundaries to each institution's power and defines limits for the extent of its authority. These boundaries include defining those who are subject to each authority, as well as the extent to which those subjects must submit. For example, while parents have the right to rule their children, they do not have the right to make their children steal.

What About Evil Rulers

Any problems arising from the abuse of authority are not the fault of God's principles, but are due to mankind's failure to function properly according to God's Word. God could at any time remove from his position of authority any individual who oversteps his boundaries, but He often allows such a one to remain in his position of power in order to discipline, or to strengthen the character of, those who are suffering under unfair rulership. The pressure that God allows to come into our lives is intended to develop our trust in God, and our dependence on His Word. Pressure is also intended to strengthen the believer's relationship with Him. God places us under the exact kind of rulership which will fulfill His plan for each of us.

The life of Joseph is an example of how God works in the life of a believer in spite of an evil ruler (See *Genesis 39-50*). Joseph was sold into slavery by his brothers to an ungodly ruler who had the power to do whatever he willed with his slave. In fact, Joseph was unjustly accused and thrown into prison. God used these evil situations to draw Joseph closer to Him. Subsequently, Joseph glorified God through the interpretation of his fellow prisoner's dreams and eventually the interpretation of Pharaoh's dreams. The pressure that Joseph withstood was rewarded—he was promoted to the second in-command of the government, his family was saved from famine, and Israel was blessed through his faithfulness. Joseph later acknowledged God's ability to work in spite of the evil intentions of others, when he said to his brothers: *"But as for you, ye thought evil against me; but God meant it unto good, to bring to pass, as it is this day, to save many people alive"* (*Genesis 50:20*). Joseph's submission to his rightful authority under the worst of conditions is a testimony to any woman in a difficult marriage.

The Authority Structure for the Institution of Marriage

The most important authority structure for a Christian woman is the institution of marriage. Since this structure governs a major portion of a woman's life, it is vital that she fully comprehends God's plan for its function.

But I would have you know that the head of every man is Christ; and the head of the woman is the man; and the head of Christ is God.

I Corinthians 11:3

This verse clearly establishes God's ordained authority structure for marriage. It reveals that the husband is the head of the family and that wives do not have equal authority in marriage. The Christian husband's authority is not without limits, however, since Christ is the ultimate head (authority) over the man. This verse also reveals that even Christ is under authority: the authority of God the Father.

It is important for a wife to understand thoroughly what God has to say about her husband's position of leadership. Otherwise, her tendency will be to overtly resist, or to quietly resent, her husband's authority. Every Christian wife answers directly to God for obeying His Word regarding submission to her husband's authority. This means that she must know the areas of her own accountability as a helpmate, and she must also know the areas in which her husband alone is accountable.

God's Word states in *Genesis 3:16*, and, *I Corinthians 11:3; Ephesians 5:23-24; I Timothy 3:2-5* and *3:12* that the husband, not the wife, is accountable to God for the rule of the home. The husband's leadership position is an obligatory responsibility. This responsibility does not leave a husband free to do as he pleases; he is accountable to God for performing his leadership duties according to God's instructions. Although a wife does not have equal earthly

42

authority with her husband, she is still personally accountable to perform her helpmate duties in accordance with God's instructions.

The authority structure of marriage should not be seen as a denouncement meant to shame women, to oppress them, or to demean their value. God did not give the husband the position of leadership because the man possesses more merit or status than the woman. Both men and women have equal spiritual status and merit before God. For instance, the biblical instructions for obtaining and maintaining a personal relationship with God are the same for both men and women. God offers each man and woman protection from eternal condemnation through the personal acceptance of Jesus Christ as his or her Saviour. Similarly, every man and woman is equally accountable to God for obedience to His Word, which includes abiding by His authority structure in marriage.

An Earthly Marriage, a Spiritual Picture

For the husband is the head of the wife, even as Christ is the head of the church; and he is the saviour of the body. Therefore as the church is subject unto Christ, so let the wives be to their own husbands in everything.

Ephesians 5:23-24

The husband's position of authority is necessary for the proper and orderly function of family government. However, this structure of family government has a far greater purpose than just the establishment of a peaceful household. Christian marriage is designed to portray to the world an image of the bond between believers and Christ. The authority structure in marriage is a picture of the spiritual authority of Christ (the husband) over believers (the wife) and of the believers' submissive bond and oneness with Christ. Presenting a Christ-like image in marriage should be the goal of every Christian couple; yet, many Christian couples today do not operate according to God's ordained authority structure. This is one reason that Christians are losing their impact on today's society. A marriage that does not operate within God's designed authority structure presents to the world a distorted view of the authority of Christ over believers.

The man's headship over his family is of such importance to God that a man desiring to hold an office in the church is biblically disqualified if he has been lax in his leadership responsibilities at home *(I Timothy 3:2-5 and 3:12)*. The proven ability of a man to lead his wife and train his children is a prerequisite to his holding a position of leadership over a portion of God's flock. Whether a husband becomes a leader in the church or not, it remains true that he must be the head of his family, generating the submission of his wife, in order to properly represent to the world Christ's headship of the church and the church's submission to Christ.

The biblical wife is privileged to play a role in the inter-linking spiritual significance of her helpmate position and Christ's submission to God the Father. When a wife grasps this spiritual significance her helpmate role takes on new meaning. While armies of Eve's rebellious daughters are being deceived into repeating Satan's call for the overthrow of God's authority,

44

she is not swayed. A biblical wife submits to her husband because she knows that God's power protects His obedient subject, and she trusts that His omniscience provides her security.

And we know that all things work together for good to them that love God, to them who are the called according to His purpose.
Romans 8:28

What shall we then say to these things? If God be for us, who can be against us?
Romans 8:31

CHAPTER VI

SUBMISSION VERSUS OBEDIENCE

Biblical submission is **not** synonymous with blind obedience! Nevertheless, even Christian women frequently define submission as slavery, meekness, or total passivity. This chapter will attempt to dispel such misconceptions about biblical submission and will reveal its spiritual significance within the husband and wife relationship. In order to understand the critical difference between submission and obedience, we need to discover the biblical definition of each word.

Obedience

God's Word uses two distinctive Greek words, one for obedience and the other for submission, when referring to the function of various subordinates within governing establishments. The Greek word *Hupakouo* is normally used in Scripture for obedience. Its technical meaning is "under the hearing of commands." A biblical command for obedience is often followed by a promise of blessing to the subject who complies, or with a warning of negative consequences to the subject who chooses noncompliance. Under the command for obedience, the subordinate is offered no alternative but to obey, nor is he allowed to debate the question of whether he should or should not obey. The appointed authority enforces compliance, executes judgment, and stands responsible for the results of his rule. The only responsibility of the subject under obedience is to do what he is told.[8]

An example of the concept of obedience (as opposed to submission) is found in *Colossians 3:22-25*. Christian slaves were instructed to remain obedient to their masters and to serve wholeheartedly, as if they were serving the Lord Himself. The following verses give us two more examples of God's use of the word "obedience." In the first passage God commands children to obey their parents.

> *Children, obey your parents in the Lord; for this is right. Honor thy father and mother (which is the first commandment with a promise), That it may be well with thee, and thou mayest live long on the earth.*   *Ephesians 6:1-3*

Notice the blessing of long life that God offers to the child who obeys his parents.

The second passage concerns the importance of obedience to God.

> *And to you who are troubled, rest with us, when the Lord Jesus shall be revealed from heaven with his mighty angels, In flaming fire taking vengeance on them that know not God, and that <u>obey not</u> the gospel of our Lord Jesus Christ; Who shall be punished with everlasting destruction from the*

presence of the Lord, and from the glory of His power. (Emphasis added)

I Thessalonians 1:7-9

Obedience to the gospel of Jesus Christ refers to the personal acceptance of Christ as the only way to eternal salvation. This example warns that the consequences for disobedience (that is, nonacceptance of Christ as Savior) will be everlasting separation from the presence and power of the Lord.

Submission

The second Greek word used in the Bible when referring to the function of subordinates is *Hupotasso* which means submission. Technically, submission means "under placement or position, status or rank." This word is used by the writers of Scripture to refer to the positions and attitudes of subjects under the authority of their government *(I Peter 2:13-15),* to believers under the teaching authority of their pastors *(Hebrews 13:17),* and of wives under the leadership of their husbands *(Ephesians 5:22).* The biblical definition of submission includes the willing and positive response of a subordinate to his rightful authority. The submissive subject **consciously and freely yields** his or her own will to the will of the authority.[9]

An example of biblical submission is Christ's submission to God the Father in the Garden of Gethsemane just prior to His death on the cross. Christ's example reveals that submission is not an act of blind obedience, but instead, it is a conscious act of a subordinate choosing to yield his will to the will of his authority.

> *And he was withdrawn from them about a stone's cast, and kneeled down, and prayed, Saying, Father, if thou be willing, remove this cup from me; nevertheless, not my will, but thine, be done.*
>
> *Luke 22:41-42*

Submission Versus Obedience

When God commands a subject to be obedient, the will of that subject is bypassed and his only choice is compliance. For example, a child is to unquestionably obey the authority of his parents, and the parents are instructed to enforce compliance, even against the child's will when necessary. However, when God commands a wife to submit to her husband's authority, He is requiring more of her than mere compliance. He is calling her to submit in a Christ-like manner.

A Christ-Like Parallel

In Chapter V, "Principles of Authority," we saw that while a wife's submission to the authority of her husband is necessary to a peaceful family life, the spiritual significance of her submission is far more important. God structured the family as a model of Christ's relationship with God the Father and of the Church's relationship with Christ.

> *But I would have you know that the head of every man is Christ; and the head of the woman is the*

50

man; and the head of Christ is God.

I Corinthians 11:3

I Peter 3 complements the spiritual picture of *I Corinthians 11:3* by revealing the Christ-like manner in which a wife is to submit to her husband.

> *In the same manner, ye wives, be in subjection to your own husbands that, if any obey not the word, they also may without the word be won by the behavior of the wives.*   *I Peter 3:1*

While some women chafe at submission and look for exceptions to the rule, the biblical woman will ask, "In what *'same manner'* do I submit?" We must refer to *I Peter 2:21-23* to understand the meaning of *"In the same manner, ye wives, be in subjection . . ."*

> *For even hereunto were ye called, because Christ also suffered for us, leaving us an example, that ye should follow his steps; Who did no sin, neither was guile found in his mouth; Who, when he was reviled, reviled not again; when he suffered, he threatened not, but committed himself to Him that judgeth righteously.*   *I Peter 2:21-23*

These verses reveal that *"in the same manner"* (*I Peter 3:1*) refers to the way Christ submitted to the plan of God. Our sinless Christ had every right to escape the injustice of being punished for sin that He did not commit, but He submitted to the worst of injustices so that He might fulfill the plan of God.

He provided a pathway to eternal salvation by means of His submission.

In the same manner as Christ, a biblical wife is to submit willingly to her husband, which is the plan of God for her life. There are at least five aspects to Christ's example of submission:

1. Christ did not sin. Submission is not just an overt act of compliance. If a wife is to submit to the authority of her husband in a Christ-like manner, she must maintain a Christ-like attitude. Biblical submission cannot be accomplished by a wife who has a sinfully bitter and angry attitude towards her subordinate role.

2. Christ was not guileful. In other words, He did not have sly motives nor any hidden agenda. Christ's submission to God the Father was not for the purpose of gaining something for Himself. A Christ-like wife will not use overt obedience as a way to manipulate her husband into doing whatever she wants.

3. Christ reviled not. When treated unjustly, Christ did not retaliate. Even while doing God's will, a submissive wife will occasionally be treated unjustly by her husband. A submissive wife will not try to "get back" at her husband for such poor treatment.

4. Christ did not threaten. Even if her husband does not handle his authority properly, a submissive wife will not threaten to withhold her favors.

5. Christ trusted God the Father. Christ was completely committed to His Father's plan and this is the reason that He was able to submit perfectly. A Christ-like wife will also submit to the authority of her husband, while she commits herself fully to *"Him that judgeth righteously"* (*I Peter 2:23*).

As you can see, the phrase *"In the same manner"* lifts the concept of a wife's submission to her husband above its earthly purpose of a peaceful family life. *"In the same manner"* highlights the importance of every believer's conscious choice to obey the will of God.

The Submissive Wife's Accountability to God

Another major difference between submission and obedience can be found in the level of responsibility that God places on a subordinate for his or her own actions and attitudes. In *Acts 5:29* we are told that obedience to God takes precedence, if there is a conflict between God's command and man's decree. A biblically submissive wife is willing to comply, but, realizing that she still remains accountable to God for personal sin, she may choose to disobey **if** her husband's request or command is a known violation of one of God's direct commands. If noncompliance is necessary, however, the biblically submissive wife continues to maintain the proper attitude of respect for her husband's leadership position and for his overall right to lead. This action might be called, "submissive noncompliance."

Submissive Noncompliance

A biblical example of submissive noncompliance is found in the *sixth chapter of Daniel*. In this passage the king made a law that *". . . whosoever shall ask a petition of any god or man for thirty days, except of thee, O king, shall be cast into the den of lions" (Daniel 6:7b).*

Obedience to the king's decree would have caused Daniel to sin against a direct command of God: *"Thou shalt have no other gods before me" (Exodus 20:3)*. Therefore, it was necessary for Daniel to disobey the king's law. However, was his disobedience an act of self-righteous rebellion, or was it submissive noncompliance? It is imperative that we examine Daniel's attitude toward his king for the answer to this question.

In the first place, Daniel maintained a close personal relationship with God, even though it meant that he had to disobey his king.

> *Now when Daniel knew that the writing was signed, he went into his house; and his windows being open in his chamber toward Jerusalem, he kneeled upon his knees three times a day, and prayed, and gave thanks before his God, as he did previously.*   *Daniel 6:10*

Secondly, there is no indication that Daniel had a rebellious or defensive attitude toward his subordinate role as a subject under a king. He previously submitted to the king's authority in all things, and he did not disobey until the king passed a new law that directly opposed God's expressed will: that believers worship Him alone, praying and giving thanks. Although Daniel knew the dire consequences of choosing to disobey in this instance, he did not do so defiantly, nor did he run away from those consequences. Daniel continued to recognize the king's right as a duly appointed authority to execute punishment.

> *Then the king commanded, and they brought Daniel, and cast him into the den of lions . . .*
> *Daniel 6:16a*

Thirdly, Daniel remained respectful of his king's position of authority. He was free from any rebellious or self-righteous attitudes before, during, and after his disobedience. Daniel's speech after God delivered him from the lions is a perfect example of willing submission to an authority in a situation requiring submissive noncompliance.

> *Then said Daniel unto the king, O king, live forever. My God hath sent His angel, and hath shut the lions' mouths, that they have not hurt me, forasmuch as before Him innocence was found in me; and also before thee, O king, have I done no hurt.*
> *Daniel 6:21 - 22*

Keep in mind that Daniel said, *"O king, live forever,"* to an authority who had just ordered his death.

Daniel's example of submission is a far cry from the defiant "I'll never let a man tell me what to do," that we hear many women say today. Such outcries usually come from women who try to justify their refusal to obey God's command to submit to their husbands by claiming that he **might** ask them to do something that would violate their personal rights. Such women lie in wait, expecting their husbands to err, so that their before-the-fact attitude of nonsubmission will be vindicated. They often fabricate "what if's" and treat the rare misuses of their husbands' authority as if they were common, everyday events. (I believe, the percentage of husbands who actually ask their godly wives to sin is very, very small. Therefore, for most women this is a moot point, born more from a desire to escape submission entirely, than a true concern over wronging God.) The attitude of women who attempt to pre-justify nonsubmission is a continuation of the garden-variety rebelliousness that has existed since the fall of mankind. By contrast, Daniel's example is a testimony of what is possible when a believer obeys God by submitting to human authorities who actually do act unrighteously.

No, obedience and submission are not synonymous. The difference, however, is not necessarily seen in one's overt actions. Obedience is an external act of compliance, while submission toward any authority is a respectful attitude that comes before, during, and after **all** actions. Where a list of rules and commands must precede obedience, submission precedes rules and supersedes law. Submission includes a woman's freedom of choice—her choice to obey God by freely yielding herself to the authority He has placed over her. It involves trust—her absolute trust in the integrity of the

God who designed her role and included submission to authority within His plan. Submission is the natural result of a biblical woman's abiding trust in God, and it is the fruit of her desire to do His Will.

Mature

Inflated

Insecure

CHAPTER VII

WHY ARE MEN SO DIFFERENT?

Men are strange creatures, aren't they? Their voices are a different pitch than women's, their bodies are shaped differently, and some deodorant ads say they even perspire differently. Also, most women think that men possess vastly inflated and overdeveloped egos. On top of everything else, they think funny too!

There certainly are more differences between the sexes than just what appears to the eye. If we compare scientific studies on the psychological and emotional make-up of the male and female, it becomes evident that there are many areas of difference. By the age of ten or eleven girls have greater verbal ability than boys, while boys excel in visual-spatial ability. It can also be observed that young boys are more aggressive both physically and verbally than girls. Male aggression usually emerges as early as social play begins, at about two or two and one half-years of age. Boys appear to be especially stimulated to bursts of high activity and competition by the presence of other boys.

It is my belief that all emotional, psychological, and physical differences between men and women were designed as a part of God's plan. He created each sex with unique bodies, distinctive thinking patterns, and specific instincts that are characteristic of the normal male and female. Such thinking patterns and instincts are not taught; instead, they are a part of the inner being of each sex.[10] It is true that, as a child grows, internal pressures (the nature to sin) and external factors (poor parental training) can seriously distort these inborn traits. Two examples are: a little girl being trained to be a "tomboy," and a "mamma's boy" being raised by a domineering mother. Nevertheless, the unique characteristics of each sex were originally meant to facilitate the fulfillment of God's design for men and women.

Women Are Responders

When the essence of the woman was removed from the original human creation, much of the responsive nature of mankind was deposited in the woman's soul. Evidence of this responsive nature exists within the emotional patterns that comprise the "mothering instinct." Women are also endowed with a depth of appreciation, sensitivity, and compassion for others. They tend to be more affectionate and to possess a greater desire to please others than do men. These and other basically feminine attributes stem from the emotionally responsive nature of the woman's soul. This natural responsiveness and its manifestations are essential for women to function as biblical helpmates and as mothers.

Men Are Initiators

Of course, men can be responsive too, but while emotional responsiveness is recognized as a trait of most women, it is less pronounced in men. The pronounced characteristic of the man's soul is the instinctive drive to initiate leadership. This initiation is manifested by self-confidence, decisiveness, and courage—necessary traits for a man to be the leader of his family. The man is also physically stronger, more aggressive, and very possessive—ideal traits for protecting and providing for his wife and family. Even the funny way men think becomes not so funny after all, but even comprehensible, when we recognize God's purpose for men. As we will see, this purpose also helps explain the reason for the male ego.

Ego

A dictionary definition of ego is: "The 'I' or self of any person; a person as thinking, feeling and willing, and distinguishing itself from the selves of others and from objects of its thought." Ego is also defined as self-esteem or self-image.[11] Ego can be positively expressed (self esteem) or negatively expressed (egotism), but its purest meaning is simply a recognition of self as distinct from others.

The way men view themselves (their egos) and how they relate to others reveal general masculine tendencies. Men are aggressive and competitive among themselves, they have a strong desire to succeed, and they instinctively desire to lead others—especially women. At an early age boys often feel protective toward their mothers and sisters, and they will respond quite seriously to the idea of being the "man of the house" while Daddy is away. Even in very young boys the idea of leading and protecting their women corresponds to their masculine egos and makes them feel valuable, needed, and good about themselves. These are just a few traits that appear to be expressions of the male ego. A man with a healthy male ego is aware of, and is comfortable with, his manliness.

A Definition for Manliness

Manliness (healthy male ego) is an important component of a man's self-image. It is the part of a man that gives him the confidence, courage, objectivity, and initiative to be a leader. Proper manliness initiates leadership. It initiates a desire to protect and provide, which are two of the ways a well-balanced man expresses his love for his wife and children. Manliness is the expression of proper manhood (the legitimate male ego) in all of its facets. The male ego and masculinity are so closely intertwined that if you destroy a man's ego, you will destroy his manliness.

Egotism

The nature to sin distorts the legitimate ego as it does every other human trait. For instance, the sin nature can distort the human ability to love and cause true love for the benefit of another to be changed into a grasping and egocentric love of self. Likewise, sin can distort the ego (male or female), and cause an individual to have an inappropriate self-image (egotism).

A man who has an inappropriate self-image will manifest either aggressive egotism or passive egotism. Some of the manifestations of aggressive egotism are exaggerated self-importance, sinful pride, and cruelty. A few of the manifestations of a man's passive egotism are passivity, insecurity, cowardliness, and a refusal to lead his wife and family.

Anyone who has watched young boys at play has observed untrained egos. Most boys begin very early in life wanting to be the "big cheese," and willing to do almost anything to top one another. They compete in everything, including which one is the biggest, and which one can talk first or loudest. Each boy's confidence is undaunted; he is positive he will be the one to win the game (by defeating others), or that his dad can whip everyone else's dad. The instinctive desire to excel is a good and natural part of a boy's maleness, but the tactics for achieving this desire are distorted by his untrained and unrestrained nature to sin, resulting in immature egotism (inappropriate self-image).

It is God's design for parents to restrain their sons' sin natures and to train them to express their natural drive to excel in acceptable ways. However, because of the lack of proper child training of boys for quite a few years, we now have a great number of distorted egos in adult men. As a result, many men today exhibit self-centered egotism, even more male egos have been damaged severely enough to produce insecurity, indecisiveness, and passivity. Passive male egos are usually the result of domineering mothers or ridiculing fathers, and then compounded by domineering wives. The chart on the next page will help you picture in your mind the difference between a healthy male ego and the distortions of egotism.

Ego

Definition: That which recognizes self as distinct from others. The male ego should be developed into maturity for the man's role of leadership and conquering of the physical world. The legitimate ego can be distorted by the human nature to sin and by poor child-training.

Expressions of Legitimate Male Ego

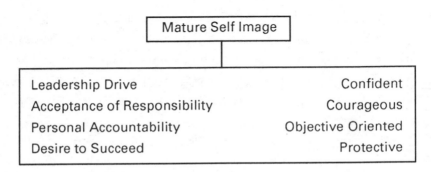

Mature Self Image

Leadership Drive	Confident
Acceptance of Responsibility	Courageous
Personal Accountability	Objective Oriented
Desire to Succeed	Protective

Two Expressions of Illegitimate Egotism

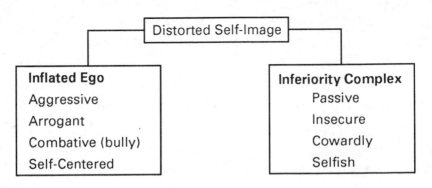

Distorted Self-Image

Inflated Ego	**Inferiority Complex**
Aggressive	Passive
Arrogant	Insecure
Combative (bully)	Cowardly
Self-Centered	Selfish

Compounded Problems

If it is true that a large percentage of today's adult men possess either damaged male egos or aggressive egotism, then it follows that most wives have inherited one of these problems. However, a wife who has a negative attitude toward even the proper male ego compounds any legitimate problem that might already exist. For example, when a normally passive husband attempts to assert himself, his wife will compound his passivity if she constantly finds fault with his efforts. In ignorance this wife discourages her husband's attempted leadership (a portion of his legitimate male ego) and pushes him farther from his manly role. Unwittingly, she destroys whatever remains of her husband's masculinity and his natural inclination to lead. This husband will eventually quit trying to lead and abdicate his leadership role entirely to his wife. Negative attitudes toward the expressions of a husband's ego are counterproductive to the role of a supportive helpmate and only tend to compound existing problems.

Samson and Delilah Allegory

The well-known Bible story of Samson and Delilah reveals much truth about the fragile nature of a man's manliness. For the sake of our discussion, we will consider Samson's hair to be analogous to the strength of his legitimate ego (his manhood). Delilah, is analogous to any woman's ability to destroy her Samson's manhood.

A man's ego is extremely vulnerable and sensitive to attacks by the Delilahs in his life (mothers, girl friends, wife). When a Delilah derides or rejects her Samson's expressions of manhood, she causes him to become discouraged and weak. Attacks can come in the form of an attitude of rejection or by sharp cutting words of belittlement. "I don't trust you." "You're so stupid when it comes to finances." "Why can't you be more like Fred?" "Your competitiveness with Jim is just silly and egotistical." These are just a few put-downs that cut straight through the heart of any Samson's ego.

Cutting off the real Samson's hair rendered him physically weak and ineffective. In the same way rejection of your husband's male ego results in the weakening of his manliness. When a man's legitimate male ego is weakened by rejection or ridicule, he will not have the strength, courage, or confidence to provide effective leadership (an expression of the male ego). Consequently, his weakened ability to lead will limit his desire to protect and provide for you. It even limits his manly expression of love. The results can be devastating. Many marriages have been destroyed by a husband having his ego flattered by another woman, **after first** having it flattened by his wife.

Attacks on your own Samson's manliness can be either an overt and vocal refusal to accept his leadership, or it can be more subtle. There are many effective ways to give your husband subtle "rejection notices." Ignore what he tells you about anything. Treat his attempts to lead as unwelcome interferences in your life. Politely listen to him, disregard his wishes, and then do whatever you feel is best. Be certain he

66

understands that, on your list of priorities, his needs come after your own. Go your own way, and "do your own thing." These are some of the ways you can effectively cut off your husband's hair (his legitimate male ego) and render him weak and powerless.

Men who submit for a long period of time to having their "hair cut off" usually become the exact opposite of what God intended. Their manly leadership drives give way to passivity, default of responsibility, fear of failure, and indecisiveness. The drive to protect women is designed to produce bravery, but when thwarted consistently, it gives way to cowardliness. When their manly drive to provide is long denied, it becomes difficult for men to accept responsibility for their own support, let alone take responsibility for the support of others.

On the other hand, a husband who has his wife's support and appreciation is encouraged to develop the more desirable traits inherent within the male ego. For instance, appreciation for a man's drive to protect women encourages him toward selflessness and bravery. When a man's drive to provide for his family is encouraged, he develops a strong sense of responsibility for others and a desire to achieve. A naturally passive man tends to become more assertive in his leadership and an aggressive man is more likely to consider the vulnerability of a submissive wife.

God made no mistake when He created the male ego. If a woman hopes to be a biblical wife, she must have the compassionate, loving spirit of one who desires to accept her man as he has been designed by God. Understanding the necessity of the legitimate male ego with all its drives and functions is one of the first steps in becoming a supportive helpmate. A wife can help repair her husband's bruised manhood (passive or aggressive), by simply being a biblical wife. She can help by appreciating and encouraging her husband's God-given drives—even if he does not always express them perfectly.

CHAPTER VIII

WHEN TWO HEADS ARE BETTER THAN ONE

Therefore shall a man leave his father and his mother, and shall cleave unto his wife; and they shall be one flesh.   *Genesis 2:24*

God's Word declares that marriage should merge two independent parts into one whole unit. However, neither part must lose its unique distinction in order to merge. In fact, the distinctions of the two make "the one" possible. Marriage is like a jigsaw puzzle with its many unique pieces. Each piece has its own distinct shape and bears a portion of the whole picture. However, the manufacturer did not intend for the puzzle pieces to remain separated, instead, he intentionally designed them to fit perfectly together. While the puzzle pieces do not lose their distinct shapes when fitted together, it is only when the pieces become one that the whole picture emerges. In the same way, God intentionally designed the male and female, distinct in shape and function, to fit together perfectly in marriage. And like the puzzle pieces, both husband and wife retain individuality and uniqueness, while portraying a whole "picture" in the unity and oneness of marriage.

In order for a husband and wife to merge into one, it is extremely important for them to understand how their different ways of thinking are important to the oneness of marriage.

Have you noticed times when you and your husband seem to be telling two different stories, even though you're talking about the same event? Do you intuitively know how people feel, while your husband thinks you're imagining things? Have you ever tried to tell your husband something exciting, only to have him become irritated with your long narration and say, "When are you going to get to the point?" Most women will say, "Yes, yes, yes! Sometimes it's as if my husband and I live on two different planets." You don't live on two different planets, but you do think on two different planes. This chapter will help you see how both your husband's and your own unique thinking patterns are needed in a marriage. (Honestly, your man's funny way of thinking wasn't created just to irritate you!)

A wife would usually accept that her husband is only half complete and needs her in order to be whole. However, this does not mean that a wife needs to mold her husband into her own image. A woman's attributes are only half complete as well; she also needs her husband in order to be whole. In a biblical marriage, the wife benefits from the way her husband thinks, and he benefits from the way she thinks. A biblical helpmate complements her husband; she does not attempt to remodel his masculine thinking into feminine thinking. Only a blend of the two unique thinking patterns, as well as all the other unique qualities of both the husband and the wife, will accomplish the oneness that God intends in marriage.

You might think that mixing the different ways men and women think is like trying to mix oil with water. This is a natural conclusion, when we don't understand how such diverse thinking patterns can actually be compatible. When a man and a woman live within God's design—the man as the head, the woman as his helpmate—their differences homogenize, and they are able to work together for a common purpose. Let's look at how these two types of thinking complement each other.

A Woman's Thinking

A woman's thinking normally includes how she **feels** about any topic. She is usually very observant of minute details and alert to the emotional reactions of others. A woman is typically quite verbal. This means that she thinks while she talks and talks while she thinks. She also tends to speak with an abundance of words. Because she is observant of details, effusive, and frequently led by her emotions, she rarely relates information in a "just-the-facts-ma'am" manner. No matter how intelligent she is, a woman's thinking is never far removed from her emotional reactions. Therefore, her presentation of data is usually dramatic, colorful, and descriptive.

A woman can have a very high IQ, but her pattern of thinking is still inseparable from her femininity. She normally displays deeply intense emotions toward the pleasure or pain of others. A woman's emotions create in her an affectionate, sensitive, and responsive nature. This sensitive nature causes her to be easily hurt when anyone, especially her father or her husband, is displeased with her.

Additionally, a woman has an inherent need for emotional, physical, and financial security. This is one reason that she appears to worry a lot. Admittedly, many women in recent generations have been disillusioned by fathers and husbands who failed to provide this essential security. A woman who has been disappointed by the men in her life may **try** to harden herself against her inherent need for security. But, the emotional need for a man to take care of her, to love her and protect her, still remains crying in her soul.

Resident within a woman's soul is a powerful desire for her man. However, I am not suggesting that a man should ever take the place of God in a woman's life. A husband is to be a complement and an earthly soul-mate, but he cannot be expected to completely fill those deeper soul needs that only God can fill. A woman can only expect to find complete acceptance through a personal relationship with God. Her entire need for security can only be found by trusting Him.

A Man's Thinking

A man tends to be less observant of the feelings of people and more attentive to issues. He is frequently less verbal than a woman and often meditates within himself rather than speaking while he thinks. A man tends to view things in a more facts-oriented manner. He is typically frank and uses short, to-the-point sentences when speaking. When a man must make a difficult decision, he does not include lengthy considerations about how people feel. He generally tries to set aside even his own feelings in order to maintain objective thinking. In this way he can be more certain that his final decision is an unbiased one. His wife may mistakenly think that he doesn't care about the effect of his decisions, or that he is insensitive to the feelings of others. Additionally, a wife may believe that her husband is shutting her out of his thoughts because he slowly meditates in silence. As a rule this is not true, but a wife may assume that it is true, if she judges her husband's way of thinking by her own thinking processes.

At first glance we might wonder how such diverse methods of thinking could ever be compatible. As we know, it is rare for either a man or a woman to understand the way the other thinks; each considers that his or her way of thinking is superior. Until men and women come to understand and appreciate the importance of their different approaches to thinking, there will always be misunderstandings between them.

Putting Two Heads Together

As we saw in Chapter VII, the different physical, emotional, and psychological make-up of each sex was designed by God as a part of His plan. In their correct positions, and with their unique attributes exercised correctly, the man and the woman are each a matching component in God's design of marriage. A woman's awareness of the feelings of others makes her more emotionally attentive as a helpmate, and her many feminine attributes prompt her towards selfless service to others. The man's objectivity makes him more adept in leadership, because his decisions are less likely to be influenced by his emotions.

Let's look at an illustration which will reveal the differences in the thinking of men and women. Through this illustration we will see how both the emotional responsiveness of the woman and the more objective approach of the man are necessary in order to fulfill God's design in marriage.

Many toddlers cry when they are first put to bed; some even scream as if they are in great pain. They will also get out of bed repeatedly, call for their mommy, ask for a drink, or use any number of other resourceful tactics in order to remain awake.

A mother naturally responds emotionally when she thinks her child is in need. This responsiveness motivates her to rush to her crying child, pick him up, and comfort him. Even if she believes that the child is not in pain, but simply trying to keep from going to bed, it is difficult for her to deny comfort. She continues to worry that **this** time he may truly be in need. She may imagine that her child is afraid and allow him to sleep with her, she may conclude that he is hungry and over-feed him, or she may allow him to stay up until he falls over from exhaustion. It is easier for a woman to give needless comfort than it is for her to deny her child's demands. This is true even when she intellectually knows that it would be better for the child if she did not to give in to his desire to stay awake.

On the other hand, a man's normal response to a child's bedtime stay-up-as-long-as-possible ritual is usually without any emotional urgency to give comfort. The typical man will look for physical reasons for the distress, and if there are none readily apparent, he will usually recognize the child's strategy as an attempt to exercise control. A man can usually make a quick decision about how to stop such control techniques and he will follow through with little emotional response to the child's tears.

A man's objectivity in child training is a necessary balance to the woman's more emotional responsiveness. His suppression of emotional response enables him to more easily consider the long-range effects of his decisions and actions, while the woman is more concerned with easing the immediate distress. This does not mean that the man is without emotions; it simply means that his emotions are restrained in favor of more objective thinking.

The mother's emotional responsiveness can be undesirable for a child's overall wellbeing, if it is untempered by the father's objectivity. This feminine responsiveness enables a woman to tend to the physical and emotional needs of others. It prompts her toward loving and tender actions which are beneficial in child-nurturing. Her sympathetic responsiveness is perfect for giving comfort and making the pain go away, but it must be mixed with objectivity when the child needs to learn the difficult lessons that are part of growing up.

Conversely, the man's objectivity alone is not sufficient to meet all of a child's needs all the time. When children are truly distressed, they need loving touches and comforting support for the proper development of their overall emotional security. Objectivity alone is cold comfort when a child truly needs sympathy or compassion. Feminine responsiveness and masculine objectivity must work **in unison** in order to provide a child with a balanced life. A child needs his mother's tender responsiveness to his present needs for emotional stability, **and** he needs his father's objectivity in order to be trained for adult life.

During a recent conversation a concerned young father put it this way: "My wife is concerned about making a healthy, happy child and she does a very good job. However, I am concerned with making a mature adult." This father recognizes that his child needs his mother's immediate nurturing, but he also recognizes that, as a father, his major concern is training the child for adulthood—a longer-ranged objective.

It is important to remember that, although a woman possesses many outstanding attributes, none of them are sufficient alone. A woman should never think that her special qualities are superior to the man's. Womanly characteristics are excellent when used as God intended, but they can also be exceedingly destructive when misapplied. Nurturing and protecting only, and instead of, objective child training will spoil a child. Responsiveness to the whims of a child will create for him an unrealistic, me-centered world. He will continue as an adult to demand instant gratification; and this self-gratification will motivate him to play on the emotions of others (especially women) in order to obtain his selfish desires.

The very attributes that make a woman warm and loving also create a susceptibility to rational blindness and emotional deception. A woman who is totally governed by her feelings is blinded to reality, and her intense emotional reactions can cause her to be susceptible to deception. Feminine qualities require balance. God gives the woman that balance through her husband's leadership. Her child will have a more balanced training for life if she does not allow her "feelings" to interfere with, or to negate, the effect of the father's more objective approach to child training.

Not only is balance needed in child training, but it is needed in all other areas of a woman's life as well. A wife's entire life will be more symmetrical when she trusts God's plan and submits to her husband's leadership. Another whole chapter could be written on how a woman's thinking helps to balance a man's thinking, but this book is not meant for men. However, even with the one-sided example of child training, the point should now be clear. When a man and a woman cooperatively "put their heads together," they balance each other's deficiencies, complement each other's strengths, and thus fulfill God's design for biblical marriage.

CHAPTER IX

WOMAN—A VERY INFLUENTIAL PERSON

Some people believe that a woman's subordinate role as helpmate prevents her from being a significant force in society. Quite the opposite is actually true. In fact, a woman's influence is so powerful that she should be required to wear a **Warning!** label. In one way or another, every woman makes an impact on her man, her children, and the society in which she lives. Her influence is either beneficial (fulfilling the plan of God) or destructive (supporting the plan of Satan). This chapter reveals several areas where a woman exerts influence—positive influence when she adheres to God's Word or negative influence when she does not. The material that is presented in this chapter will help dispel the myth that the woman's subordinate role is not meaningful. It will also warn of the significant damage that can be caused when a woman chooses to live outside God's design.

A Woman's Influence on Her Children

A well-known adage is, "The hand that rocks the cradle rules the world." Until quite recently, mother and the home were virtually synonymous in the minds of people. Memories of the childhood home usually centered around Mom—how she cooked, soothed pain, and especially the moral standards that she taught. A mother's influence over her children's attitudes about themselves and others, about authorities, and about God lasts a lifetime. In the Word of God a king spoke of his mother's influence.

> *The words of King Lemuel, the prophecy that his mother taught him.*   *Proverbs 31:1*

The Bible states that the mother's teaching of children has equal standing with the father's teaching. That teaching becomes the standard by which a new generation will live.

> *My son, hear the instruction of thy father, and forsake not the law of thy mother; for they shall be an ornament of grace unto thy head, and chains about thy neck.*   *Proverbs 1:8-9*

Most Christians today are saddened by our nation's departure from God's Word and from basic morality. It is not coincidental that this decline in morality happened shortly after a large percentage of mothers entered the workplace (from about 1940). As a result of working outside the home, many of today's Christian mothers are regularly abdicating their child-training responsibilities to secular daycare centers and public schools. The secular world teaches its own standards and in many cases these standards are in direct opposition to Christian principles. While the secular world rocks the cradle, absentee mothers are losing daily opportunities for the moral training of their children. This situation is producing an atmosphere conducive to the influence of satanic immorality and godless autonomy.

Deterioration of moral standards in our nation began with the neglect by Christian parents of properly training past generations. Restoration of morality can begin only when Christian mothers return to the training of their own children. Christian women, who love God more than the world, can provide a home environment where the laws of God flourish and where satanic influence is exposed and countered. I believe that just one woman who understands biblical principles can begin with her own children, and by training them in those biblical principles, can influence the revival of an entire nation.

A Woman's Influence as a Teacher of Other Women

The aged women likewise . . . That they may teach the young women . . .   *Titus 2:3a & 4a*

Older women teaching younger women is an influence that is desperately needed today. For several generations the teaching of biblical womanhood to our daughters has been seriously neglected in Christian homes. Two basic reasons for this neglect have been mothers who were ignorant of biblical principles themselves and mothers who, by pursuing their own goals outside the home, found no time for training their daughters. The only marriage training many of our modern daughters ever receive is in their school home economics and sex education courses, from pulp magazines and the entertainment media, and from their peers. The emphasis of school courses and the entertainment media is primarily controlled by secular thought and includes no biblical principles whatsoever. Likewise, a young woman's peers are usually as ignorant of biblical principles as she is herself and can offer only youthfully self-centered advice.

God's purpose in commanding the older woman to teach the younger woman is so *". . . that the Word of God be not blasphemed."* through the younger woman's manner of life *(Titus 2:5b)*. But today the Word of God is being blasphemed because many adult daughters follow secular advice about marriage, rather than looking to the Word of God. This secular advice frequently encourages them to live in ways which directly oppose the Word of God, including immorality and divorce on demand.

Marriage difficulties and divorce cause immense pain for everyone concerned—the husband, the wife, and especially the children. Many churches today are responding to this intense human agony by offering codependency programs and other psychologically-based classes. Unfortunately, this solution is similar to treating the symptoms of an illness, rather than eliminating the cause of the disease. God's method of having older women teaching younger women is a preventative measure that helps to keep the patients healthy, thereby preventing serious epidemics. Churches would help Christian marriages most by identifying and developing qualified older women to teach younger women about biblical womanhood and marriage before the problems begin.

God has given the biblical criteria by which we can identify the qualified older woman. Before she is allowed to teach, the older woman's life-resume should reflect the following attributes and qualifications:

The aged women, likewise, that they be in behavior
as becometh holiness, not false accusers, not given
to much wine, teachers of good things. . ..

Titus 2:3

The "good things" that are to be taught include teaching younger women:

. . . to be sober-minded, to love their husbands, to love their children, to be discreet, chaste, keepers at home, good, obedient (literally, subject) *to their own husbands. . .*

Titus 2:4b-5a

As a child of God, you should evaluate anyone who teaches you by these biblical standards. Does her teaching reflect the "good things" of *Titus 2:4-5*? Does she honor or blaspheme the Word of God? If you follow her suggestions will they cause a growth of love and understanding between you and your husband, or will they increase alienation and cause dissension? Subjecting our modern "experts" to this close scrutiny will disqualify a great many of them, thereby diminishing the harm that could be inflicted by their blasphemous advice.

A Woman's Influence over Her Husband

As we have seen a woman can be a substantial influence on her children and on younger women. However, perhaps the greatest impact a woman makes is on her husband. A wife's influence is felt in four basic areas of her husband's life:

85

1. On Her Husband's Masculinity

On a recent Saturday morning a husband and wife in my neighborhood were holding a garage sale. People were milling around and the husband was standing off to the side talking to a friend. A customer approached the husband and made a lowered bid for an end table. Upon overhearing her husband agree to the ten dollar reduction, the wife called from across the yard, "What did you let that go for? Oh Jim, how stupid!" Jim looked at his friend and shrugged his shoulders in embarrassment. If this scene had been in a movie, some appropriate music would have signaled that this was a significant moment. As it was, I may have been the only one who heard the first notes of the death march for Jim's masculinity.

Without realizing that her words cut like a chisel, the wife at the garage sale chipped off a piece of her husband's manhood. Unknowingly, she helped her husband to lose interest in making further decisions. Jim most likely played it safe for the remainder of the day and deferred all questions to his wife. He may have eventually gone indoors to watch TV and left her to manage on her own. By the time she closed the garage sale, the wife felt totally exhausted and exasperated because she had had to do everything herself. Jim's wife unwisely defeated the purpose of a helpmate when she shamed her husband. Instead of encouraging him to make decisions, she helped him to retreat from decision-making. I wonder if the loss of ten dollars was worth the damage to Jim's manhood.

This story is all too typical of the negative influence many modern wives inflict upon their husbands' manhood. The non-biblical wife is usually unaware that she can mentally and emotionally abuse her husband's masculinity when she treats him as a child, complains about his decisions, or corrects him in public. This type of wife frequently blames her husband for the weaknesses that she reinforces with her own words and actions. Rarely does a wife realize that the quality of her husband's leadership is directly proportional to the health of his manhood. Damage a husband's manhood and he will begin to lose the desire (and confidence) to be a responsible husband. Conversely, protect and support his manhood and he becomes encouraged to be a better leader, provider, and protector.

2. On Her Husband's Initiative to Succeed in Life

It is not a misnomer when some husbands proudly refer to their wives as their "better half." A husband with this attitude is aware that his wife's influence adds to his life a previously missing ingredient. Without her he would have less reason to bear up under the hardships and burdens of a man's responsibilities. Her demonstration of trust in his ability to succeed and her appreciation of his efforts strengthen his resolve to be victorious in life's battles. The biblical woman is truly her husband's "better half," as well as his loyal and compassionate friend.

On the other hand, the wife who refuses to fulfill the intended design of helpmate abandons her husband to fight his battles alone. Without a helpmate fit for him, he is vulnerable to a multitude of difficulties. Instead of his helpmate easing the pain of life, her indifference increases his suffering; instead of building his confidence, her lack of support weakens his morale. Rather than assuaging his doubts, her distrustful criticisms increase his insecurity and destroy his initiative. When a wife is a negative influence on her husband, she becomes the "old ball and chain," rather than his "better half."

3. On Major Leadership Decisions

Some women become very confused concerning decision-making. They think that the "older woman" is saying that every decision must be made by the husband while the wife remains completely silent. We are not saying that a wife must never make decisions, but that there is a difference between **leadership decisions** and **subordinate decisions**. Before we look at a woman's influence on her husband's leadership, let's first establish the difference between these two types of decisions.

Leadership decisions concern those issues that have a major impact on the entire family. A matter that requires a final determination before action can take place is within the realm of a husband's leadership. Examples of major decisions that a husband should make are: determining where the family should live, where they attend church, decisions about job changes, establishing a budget, and setting the standards for child training. These examples are all within the husband's role and area of responsibility as leader, protector, and provider.

Subordinate decisions concern how to follow through and successfully implement the policies of the leader, while remaining within the established guidelines. Examples of a wife's subordinate decisions are: determination of how to run the home, finding ways to live within the budget, and actually training the children within the standards set. As long as the wife's decisions are within the guidelines set by her husband, she has tremendous freedom of choice. For instance, setting the family food budget is a policy decision, but planning the menus and determining where to find the best prices are decisions within the realm of subordinate follow-through. A wife may need to seek her husband's approval before purchasing a major appliance, but she should not need to check with her husband before purchasing every loaf of bread.

Even though a husband is ultimately responsible for leadership decisions, a wife should remember that she is always in a position to influence those decisions. A wife who knows her husband is assertive and secure in his role as leader may freely express her views and preferences during pre-decision discussions. The wife of a husband who biblically leads his family, can relax in the confidence that her husband will weigh her ideas carefully before making a major decision. Unfortunately, few wives in today's world have reason to be confident in their husband's ability to make wise decisions. Therefore, it is a common belief that a wife should exert a strong influence whenever she believes her husband's leadership is unwise or weak. However, this belief is counterproductive to the correct role of helpmate and only assures the continuation of poor leadership.

Dangerous Influence

In order to assure that her influence is beneficial and constructive, a wife must use her influence with great discernment. For instance, a persuasive wife is in danger of misusing her power to influence if her husband is less assertive than she is. A discerning wife, who knows her husband might prefer to escape leadership responsibilities, should be especially careful to refrain from forcefully expressing her opinions. This is particularly true if she has a tendency to instigate debates over every decision, or if she finds that her husband is easily overpowered by her persuasive arguments. When a woman uses her powers of persuasion to consistently back her husband down from his final decisions, she discourages him from developing his full leadership potential and can cause him to become inactive as a leader. Many modern-day husbands have been persuaded to become silent partners in their marriages by these nonsubmissive wives.

I realize that many women will feel frustrated at the idea of withholding their opinions from their less assertive husbands. "I can't just keep my mouth shut and play like I'm stupid," is how a great many women express their rejection of this concept. Before you throw out the whole concept, however, please consider that this is probably how Rebekah, Isaac's wife, felt.

God told Rebekah, while she was pregnant with the twins, that the older son, Esau, would serve the younger son, Jacob. This promise was opposite the normal system of family

90

rulership by the eldest son. Additionally, Isaac favored Esau. Because of these apparent problems, Rebekah did not believe she could trust God to work through her husband to do what He had promised. Therefore, she urged her favorite son, Jacob, to deceive his father in order to steal his brother's blessing *(Genesis 27:1-40)*. The results of Rebekah's influence were disastrous to the family. Esau was filled with jealous hatred for his brother *(Genesis 27:41* and *28:6-9)*, and Jacob had to flee the country to escape his brother's anger *(Genesis 27:42-45)*. It is quite possible that Rebekah's interference caused her never to see her favorite son again!

When solutions to problems appear to take forever, a woman must be especially careful of her power to influence her husband. A woman typically wants decisions made and problems solved—NOW! When problems loom and solutions are not forthcoming, it isn't unusual for a woman to become quite impatient. But, if she attempts to force her husband into a premature action she could easily create a disastrous situation. Abraham's wife is a perfect illustration of a wife who became impatient while waiting for something to happen. Sara was convinced that she was barren forever, so she suggested that Abraham should have a child by her handmaiden Hagar, in order to fulfill God's prophecy. Sara, like Rebekah, thought God's plan needed her intervention. The hideous consequences that came upon their household when Abraham followed his wife's leadership are recorded in *Genesis 16* and *21:9-21*. The examples of Rebekah's and Sara's interfering influence over their husbands prove that it is only prudent for a wife to be concerned about the possible long-ranged effect of her suggestions—before she speaks.

91

Correct Influence

Whether your husband is nonassertive, assertive, or somewhere in between, the one guideline that will help you keep from exercising incorrect influence on him is your faith in biblical submission. As long as a wife is not argumentative (repetitive debating), resistive (refusing to accept his final decision), or rebellious (defiant and insubordinate), she can speak her opinions (once, not thrice) during the decision making process. During these discussions a wife's submissive attitude should always be evident. She should only present her objections, or possible problems, to the extent that she has fully communicated them. Her husband should never be caused to doubt that she is willing to abide by his final decision.

Please do not fall for the popular misconception that a woman's subordinate role leaves her weak and defenseless. Since it is God's design that a wife should submit to her husband, there is considerable power backing up her biblical submission. This does not mean that God will always prevent a husband from making leadership errors. But, God often uses a husband's error in judgment as a training exercise to improve his leadership in the future. A wife can relax in the knowledge that God will provide for her while He is training her husband. Therefore, it is not the submissive wife who is defenseless; it is the nonsubmissive wife who is without defense. Within God's well-fortified citadel of biblical marriage, a submissive wife is provided for today, as well as tomorrow.

4. On Spiritual Issues

More women attend church, read Christian books, teach Sunday School, and ask spiritual questions, than do men. Why, then, does God say, *"And if they* (wives) *will learn anything, let them ask their own husbands at home. . ."* *(I Corinthians 14:35a)?*

When the serpent approached Eve, it was not because she was less spiritual than Adam, but because she was more emotionally responsive to misdirection. A modern woman's susceptibility to misdirection is the same as Eve's, no matter how logical or brilliant she may be. It is partially **because** of the woman's interest in knowledge that God directs the husband to be the spiritual head of the family. Remember, a woman's weaknesses are pride and an insatiable desire for knowledge, both of which make her easily deceived. The husband's responsibility for spiritual leadership is a grace gift given by God for the wife's protection from deception.

By God's design the husband is the spiritual head of his family. However, his wife has a direct and powerful influence on his leadership. A woman who is more eager for spiritual information than her husband should not nag or push him into studying the Word of God. She is never to usurp her husband's leadership position, nor is she to be his teacher.

> *Let the woman learn in silence with all subjection.*
> *But I permit not a woman to teach, nor to usurp*
> *authority over the man, but to be in silence.*
> *I Timothy 2:11-12*

A wife is to ask her husband questions and then listen to his reply, trusting that God will supply the answers. God can reward the biblical woman's obedience to His Word by using her positive example as a powerful spiritual influence on her husband. This simple method is how God can use a biblical wife to encourage and strengthen her husband in his spiritual leadership.

> *In the same manner, ye wives, be in subjection to your own husbands that, if any obey not the word, they also may without the word* (literally, without a word) *be won by the behavior of the wives. While they behold your chaste conduct, coupled with fear.* I Peter 3:1-2
> (The fear referred to in context is of God, not a fear of husbands.)

Concern about their husbands' poor leadership skills prompts many women to disobey God's design for marriage in the area of spiritual leadership. No woman, however, has more power to protect herself from the consequences of poor leadership than does God. Nor does any woman possess God's ability to weave together *"all things" (Romans 8:28)* into results that are beneficial for all those involved. Trusting God enough to obey Him makes a woman the recipient of an invincible, heavenly advocacy. A woman who insists on trying to protect herself by influencing her husband unwisely cuts off this invincible power.

> *For after this manner in the old time the holy women also, who trusted in God, adorned*

94

themselves, being in subjection unto their own husbands. Even as Sarah obeyed Abraham, calling him lord; whose daughters ye are, as long as ye do well, and are not afraid with any terror.

I Peter 3:5-6

This verse promises that a wife doesn't need to fear the results of her husband's decisions—even when they are wrong! A woman who understands these principles realizes that her influence is spiritually strongest when it is personally weakest.

Warning!

Many of today's women feel personally insulted when they are taught that their husbands are to be the spiritual heads of their families. These women usually declare themselves spiritually independent of their husbands. The results of this stance are disastrous to the women, to their husbands, and to their families. Let's look at just a few of these harmful results.

A woman who believes that her own intellect can protect her from falsehoods is deceived already. There is no intellect great enough to declare itself exempt from God's design. A woman deceived into believing that she is superior to God's design will inevitably become a prideful woman—rebellious to all authority and arrogant in her knowledge of biblical data.

Knowledge puffeth up, but love edifieth.

I Corinthians 8:1b

A proud self-righteous woman often becomes the wife who uses her religion as a weapon. She "preaches" at her husband and showers him with condemnation for his many "sins."

When a wife becomes proud in her own supposed spiritual autonomy, her husband's resolve to improve his spiritual knowledge may be weakened. It is easier for him to "save face" by pretending not to care about spiritual things, than to compete with a wife who uses her vast vocabulary and abundant knowledge of biblical facts as a club over his head. When his confidence in himself is shattered, he is less interested in protecting his wife from false teachings (she wouldn't listen anyway). Furthermore, this husband will frequently take no interest in church, maintaining that church is for women and children only. A preponderance of women as spiritual leaders of their families causes the church to suffer from a lack of male leadership. Sadly, this type of wife will wish she could influence her husband toward spiritual things, completely unaware that she is his excuse to default his responsibility as spiritual head of his family.

In Conclusion

To be certain that her influence is beneficial to those she loves, a biblical woman must practice discernment and employ wisdom. Among her standards of conduct should be self-control and avoidance of manipulative tactics. A biblical woman knows that a self-important image is not a Christ-like image; therefore, she submits herself to God's will.

There are many benefits when a biblical helpmate influences her husband positively. Freedom from competition for the leadership position at home makes a husband a more confident employee in the workplace. His desire to lead well promotes a desire for self-improvement. The husband who has a biblical helpmate will often begin to develop his potential for leadership and for service in the church. As a result, he and his wife become an excellent Christian testimony, which glorifies God and prevents His Word from being blasphemed. This couple's unity provides their children with a stable and secure home environment. Furthermore, because God protects those who honor Him, the whole nation benefits from biblically functioning homes. All these blessings are possible when a woman trusts God enough to function as a biblical helpmate and to influence her husband only in ways that bring glory and honor to Him.

CHAPTER X

A ROLE MODEL FOR BIBLICAL WOMANHOOD

In the previous nine chapters, I have attempted to present some basic principles for biblical womanhood. *Proverbs 31:10-31* can be said to be the condensed version of those principles, and the woman described there is the epitome of biblical womanhood. As we come to the close of *Section One: Foundations*, it seems fitting to introduce the woman who has been the biblical woman's role model for thousands of years.

Unfortunately, many women treat the *Proverbs 31* woman as a relic of the past—ideal, perhaps, but certainly unrealistic for the complexities of modern living. Even among Christian women, the consensus of today's thinking is that it is no longer practical for a woman to trust her physical, mental, emotional, and financial well-being to the same life-style that this woman represents. I exhort the Christian woman, however, to remember that the faithfulness of God and the permanency of His Word dictates that *Proverbs 31* is as relevant today as it was the day it was written.

> *Heaven and earth shall pass away, but my words shall not pass away.*   *Matthew 24:35*

Christian women can still confidently look at the *Proverbs 31* woman as their role model for biblical womanhood. The following is an interview in which the *Proverbs 31* woman is asked some questions about issues that pressure women today. Her responses are paraphrased, but the verses that relate to her answers are in parentheses so that you may confirm their accuracy.

Modern Questions for the Proverbs 31 Woman

1. **Don't you feel your talents are smothered by your subordinate role?**

   "No, I work with delight (not grudgingly)" *(verse 13)*. "I am satisfied and fulfilled for I sense that my gain is good" *(verse 18)*. "I have strength and dignity and smile (have no fear) at the future" *(verses 21 & 25)*. "All that I do shows my willingness to be of service to my household and to others" *(verses 15, 16, 18-22, 24, 27-31)*.

2. **Don't you feel that you have lost all personal identity and have become merely an extension of your husband?**

   "No, I am worth far more than jewels" *(verse 10)*. "I am strong" *(verse 17)*. "I have compassion" *(verse 20)*. "I am wise and kind" *(verse 26)*. "Strength and dignity are part of my character and my family's future is secure" *(verses 11 & 25)*. "I am praised, honored, and respected by my children and my husband" *(verse 28)*.

100

"My husband considers me the most wonderful woman of all women" *(verse 29)*.

3. **Haven't you stifled your own personality and neglected the development of your own intelligence through mindless drudgery?**

"No, not at all. I have a very keen business sense" *(verses 13-24)*. "When I speak, it is with wisdom. I teach kindness. My soul is exposed by what and how I speak" *(verse 26)*. "I use my intelligence to serve my household well." *(verses 15, 16, 18-22, 27-31)*.

4. **Aren't you just a lady of leisure—lazy, kept, spending your time watching soaps, doing useless chores, instead of accomplishing something of value for society?**

"What a strange question! I am not a burden to my husband because my deeds cause him only good and not evil." (i.e. not an embarrassment to him, do not cause him misery, distress, injury, or wrong) *(verse 12)*. "I am a hard worker. I serve my children and my husband. I also serve my community" *(verses 13-22, 24, 25, 27)*. "My husband does not need to worry about what is going on at home. He can trust me and attend to his business. Because I do my job he lacks nothing" *(verse 11)*. "I delight in my work" *(verse 13)*. "I produce by service (the hands) and I am praised in the city" *(verse 31)*.

5. **Don't you feel the need to leave those boring, repetitive, futile domestic chores and become a complete, valuable person? Can't you think of the future and what might happen if you suddenly had to support yourself?**

"Absolutely not! My trust is in God, not in myself. I support my husband and do my part within the boundaries of my role" *(All verses)*. "Together we prosper and are praiseworthy" *(verses 23 & 31)*. The underlying motive of all that I do is service for others, not self-service" *(verses 11, 12, 23, 28, & 29)*. "Because I do the will of the Lord I do not feel insecure, fearful, or in need of protecting myself" *(verses 18, 21, 25, & 31)*.

Proverbs 31 is a declaration that there is no higher calling for a woman than that of wife and mother. The *Proverbs 31* woman also had the freedom to develop business interests. These interests did not interfere with her main roles as helpmate to her husband, mother of their children, or keeper of their home. All her activities were interrelated with her home, and they were extensions of her role as a biblical woman. The *Proverbs 31* woman's motivations and accomplishments reflect the revealed will of God for womanhood. She is the forerunner of biblical womanhood and her example exhorts generations of believing women to follow her lead.

Throughout history other women have chosen different paths and have even been lauded as role models for younger generations. Many have achieved fame and fortune, only to find that their achievements are void of fulfillment. Remarks that a famous movie star made during her lifetime describe just such an emptiness. The following statements were printed by a newspaper on the day following Ava Gardner's death.

Ava Gardner speaks out: "I act for money, no other reason. Since I made my first picture in 1941, I haven't done a thing that is worthwhile."

"I have never enjoyed making films, and I don't like being a so called film star. I haven't the emotional make-up for it, nor the love of exhibitionism. I am much too shy." Gardner once said she grew up hoping to find "one good man I could love and marry and cook for and make a home for, who would stick around for the rest of my life. I never found him. If I had, I would have traded in my career in a minute."[12]

I feel an overwhelming sadness when reading Ava Gardner's assessment of her life. Her expression of emptiness and lack of fulfillment stands in sharp contrast to the fullness of the life of the *Proverbs 31* woman. Gardner would have forsaken all her achievements for what the *Proverbs 31* woman had. It is too late for Ava Gardner, but perhaps her words will help warn other women—before they suffer the same type of loss and before the end of their lives reflect the same despair.

A woman who devotes her life to living biblical womanhood chooses the most important career that any woman can possibly pursue. The biblical woman is the only one who can support her husband, and so encourage him to be everything God intends for him to be. A biblical wife, by her submission, can be a testimony of Christ's selfless sacrifice in His submission to the plan of God the Father. Her success as a biblical wife is a confirmation of God's provision, and her submission in marriage is a picture of the church's relationship to Christ. Her dedication to her family, guided by her knowledge of the principles of biblical womanhood, will provide the stability her children need as preparation for meeting the challenges of adulthood. A woman can search to the ends of the earth for a way to serve God, but she will never find a higher calling, or a more fulfilling one, than that of helpmate to her husband.

CHAPTER XI

PUTTING IT ALL TOGETHER

Our study of biblical womanhood to this point has established a firm foundation of biblical principles on which to build a marriage. We have seen how the woman was created as one-half of the original creation that God named "mankind." The woman and the man are incomplete without each other (except for the specialized exception of celibacy, *I Corinthians 7:7)*. We have discovered that God's purpose for the woman is to be a helpmate (aide, assistant, supporter, backer, etc.) to her man. We have been reminded that she was made from the man and for the man—not merely for the man's pleasure, but also for the fulfillment of God's plan. The woman was created after the man, but this does not meant that she is second best. Woman is a special, and a specialized, creation. She is to be the mate and creative helper of her husband. As life-giver and nurturer of their children, the woman also plays a singular role in the Divine directive to populate the earth.

Why, then, have so many women today rejected this grand design? Deception! The Bible says that in the last days people will be *". . . without natural affection"* *(II Timothy 3:3)*. They will be self-centered and unloving. Can you think of any better example of this lack of natural affection than the increasing number of women today who are not only leaving their husbands to follow their own dreams, but who are also abandoning their children? It is as if these women have been bewitched away from their instinctive devotion to family. The truth is that Satan has been as successful in the mass deception of modern-day women as he was with Eve in the garden. He has appealed to the woman's lust for acquisition of knowledge and to her prideful desire for autonomy—and the woman has fallen again. Through all forms of the entertainment media Satan **constantly** bombards today's women with his party line:

> "Knowledge equals freedom"
> "Be your own authority"
> "Women are superior to men"
> "You don't need a man to tell you what to do"
> "You are being kept from good things by men"

As went Eve, so goes an ever-increasing number of modern-day women, including far too many Christian women.

We have studied the consequences of Eve's fall on all women—great difficulty in child bearing and a strong desire to control her man. And, apparently worst of all, the husband was given authority over the wife. Consequently, the one who desired to be autonomous even from God must now submit to another mere human. These consequences could all add up to be an almost unbearable curse for Eve and her daughters.

But, God is love, not only justice. In His grace, His plan provides bountiful blessings for the wife through her husband's position of leadership. Her husband is to provide vision for the marriage, he is to shield her from deception and protect her physically, and he is to provide for her and their children. She, in turn, can enjoy oneness of soul with her husband, a personal sense of security, and a feeling of fulfillment, when she follows God's plan for her life.

We have also studied the most difficult concept for willful creatures to accept—authority. All of mankind would find life easier, if they understood and trusted God's provision of human authority. Proper authority provides structure, order, safety, maximum freedom for the individual, and peace. A wife can trust her husband's leadership because of her knowledgeable trust in God, not because of blind belief in another fallible human. The submission of Jesus Christ to the Father's will is the model for the biblical wife's submission to her husband.

We have learned the crucial difference between submission and obedience. We found that a wife, on occasion, can obey her husband, but still not be submissive. We learned that the submission God expects from us as wives is the voluntary yielding of our wills; it is not the unquestioning obedience expected of a child or a slave. We discovered the safety valve of "submissive noncompliance," which is to protect us from being pressured into sin by our authorities.

We have also examined some of the unique factors that make the man so different from the woman. The major factor is the male ego. Rather than some horrible drive used to dominate women, this ego is found to be essential to proper manliness, but it is very fragile. The biblical woman will become an expert on her man's ego—how not to harm it, and how properly to encourage his manhood. Understanding the necessity of the legitimate male ego, with all its drives and functions, is one of the first steps in becoming a supportive helpmate.

If the male ego wasn't a major enough difference between men and women, we also learned that men think differently than women. The man is objective and data-oriented in his thinking, while the woman thinks in terms of relationships, emotions, and pictures. Incompatible as these two may appear to be, they merge in a mature marriage to produce a balanced viewpoint in all areas of life. Like two interlocking parts of a puzzle: apart, they are incomplete; but together they combine to produce a whole that is greater than its parts—a marriage.

Next, we discovered the tremendous influence every woman has over those around her. Her influence can be either beneficial or destructive to other women, to her children, and especially to her husband. We studied the four main areas where a woman influences her husband, either positively or negatively. These areas are: his manhood, his family leadership, his decision-making, and his spiritual leadership. It is easy to see that a woman does not need to exert herself forcefully in order to make her mark upon the world. In fact, she may need to restrain herself in order to make her best contribution.

Finally, we have seen the spiritual and earthly importance that God designed for biblical womanhood. The woman is not only important to her husband, she is crucial to her children and can be a positive testimony to all those around her. She can also express her creativity and find great fulfillment in her unique role. The final conclusion can only be that biblical womanhood is indeed a woman's highest calling.

SECTION II

OPPOSITIONS TO BIBLICAL WOMANHOOD

INTRODUCTION

Section I sets forth the complete biblical position on womanhood and marriage from the woman's perspective. Most Christian women today have been taught many of these same biblical concepts in their churches. Why then do so many Christian women continue to live their lives imitating the world's standards instead of God's? There are at least two reasons a Christian woman might live her life in opposition to God's design for womanhood.

* She has been deceived by vain (empty, deceitful) philosophies.

* She is governed by her own faulty thinking patterns.

Oppositions to Biblical Womanhood is designed to alert you to the antibiblical position of today's vain philosophies concerning women. This section will help to identify the lies that can lead you into vain philosophies and show you how to defuse their effect in your life.

This section will also analyze several faulty thinking patterns that can block women from the truth about womanhood and show you how to replace such faulty thinking with God's way of thinking. Understanding the concepts presented in Section II can help to protect you from being used by Satan or from being controlled by your own sin nature.

Tower of Babel

CHAPTER XII

VAIN PHILOSOPHIES

Vanity of vanities, saith the Preacher, vanity of vanities; all is vanity.　　　　　*Ecclesiastes 1:2*

The thing that hath been, it is that which shall be; and that which is done, is that which shall be done; and there is no new thing under the sun.
　　　　　　　　　　　　Ecclesiastes 1:9

There is nothing new under the sun! All the "new" humanistic philosophies and psychological theories that attempt to explain who we are and how we should live are simply modern versions of the old counterfeit philosophy with which Satan deceived Eve. Men and women have always had to choose between God's philosophy of life and Satan's counterfeit philosophies. Each human being, from Adam and Eve to yourself, must choose which philosophy they will listen to and follow.

How to Identify Satanic Philosophies

Beware lest any man spoil you through philosophy and vain deceit, after the tradition of men, after the rudiments of the world, and not after Christ.
　　　　　　　　　　　　Colossians 2:8

There is only one **true** philosophy of life and it is revealed by the Word of God. However, there are **many** false philosophies. The believer needs to realize that every philosophy that does not come from God ultimately comes from Satan. At the beginning of creation Satan rejected God, thus establishing the basis of all vain philosophies. As it was in the beginning, so it is today—modern vain philosophies still reject God and His authority. Whether it is humanism, feminism, or any other ism, these vain philosophies attempt to explain the meaning of life apart from God.

The human authors of anti-God philosophies are often considered by themselves and others to be original thinkers. However, like Satan, these human philosophers base their systems of thinking on the rejection of God and on the denial of the absolute authority of His Word. When human philosophies reject God, their founders are not really being the brilliant original thinkers that they believe themselves to be. Instead, they are just following the vain philosophy founded by Satan—the father of lies.

Jesus told the religious leaders of His day that they were following the vain philosophy of Satan:

> *Why do ye not understand my speech? Even because ye cannot hear my word, Ye are of your father the devil, and the lusts of your father ye will do. He was a murderer from the beginning, and abode not in the truth, because there is no truth in him. When he speaketh a lie, he speaketh of his own; for he is a liar, and the father of it.*
> *John 8:43-44*

Vain philosophies can be identified in several ways. The most obvious sign is a beginning premise that rejects God. But the more subtly-deceptive tenets of vain philosophies can also be recognized by the knowledgeable student of God's Word. The basic doctrines of false philosophies follow the same pattern that Satan utilized when he deceived Eve in the garden. The pattern of Satanic philosophies begins by suggesting **doubt** that God's Word is literal and so they urge us to reject biblical principles and standards. Vain philosophies also contain messages that emotionally incite us to feel **discontent** with the biblical way of life. And finally, a satanic philosophy encourages its followers to live lifestyles of **disbelief** that are in direct rebellion against God and His Word. *

An Example of a "Modern" Vain Philosophy

An example of a "modern" philosophy of life that follows the satanic pattern is the women's liberation movement, now known as the feminist movement. Sometime in the early 1970's this popular movement came to my attention and I asked myself, "Is the philosophy compatible with God's Word, or is it a deceitful philosophy conceived and promoted by Satan?"

---

* I am indebted to Pastor Carl Denti for this insight. He is the teacher whose Bible research discovered that Satan's philosophy consists of a sophisticated structure that first causes **doubt,** then leads to **discontent,** and finally leads to **disbelief** or rebellion.

A study of the authors and promoters of the feminist movement, along with a review of their basic philosophical tenets, immediately revealed the original source of this "new" philosophy. I discovered that, the feminist movement promotes **doubt** about God's way, **discontent** with being a wife and mother, and **disbelief** of God's order for marriage and the family. The following are just a few of the many statements by the leaders and promoters of the feminist movement that demonstrate the anti-God origin of this vain philosophy.

> Paul Kurtz, author of the *Humanist Manifesto II*, editor-in chief of Prometheus Books (Humanism's most important publishing house) and editor of *Free Inquiry* magazine:

> "The feminist movement was begun and has been nourished by leading humanist women."[13]

Mr. Kurtz specifically mentions Elizabeth Cady Stanton, Betty Friedan (Author of *The Feminine Mystique*, 1963, and Humanist of the Year 1975), Gloria Steinem, and Simone de Beauvoir. His acknowledgement that the feminist movement and humanism are philosophically linked is very important to note, because humanists emphatically reject God and they believe that mankind is its own God.

> Julian Huxley (1888-1975), another well known humanist and evolutionist, defined a humanist as follows:

120

"I use the word 'Humanist' to mean someone who believes that man is just as much a natural phenomenon as an animal or a plant, that his body, his mind, and his soul were not supernaturally created but are all products of evolution, and that he is not under the control or guidance of any supernatural Being or beings, but has to rely on himself and his own powers."[14]

Elizabeth Cady Stanton, recognized by Mr. Paul Kurtz as a fellow humanist, was one of the leading organizers for the *Seneca Falls Declaration on Women's Rights*, July 19, 1848, and author of *Eighty Years and More* in 1898. She writes:

"The memory of my own suffering has prevented me from ever shadowing one young soul with the superstitions of the Christian religion."[15]

Annie Laurie Gaylor, a feminist writer in *The Humanist* (This magazine is an official bimonthly organ for humanist leader's articles) writes:

"Let's forget about the mythical Jesus and look for encouragement, solace, and inspiration from real women.. . . Two thousand years of patriarchal rule under the shadow of the cross ought to be enough to turn women toward the feminist 'salvation' of the world."[16]

Gloria Steinem, editor of *Ms. magazine*, author of *Outrageous Acts and Everyday Rebellions* in which she admired Elizabeth Cady Stanton for her rejection of biblical womanhood[17], and herself a vocal leader in the present day feminist movement, believes we should:

". . . raise our children to believe in human potential, not God."[18]

Sol Gordon, another writer for *The Humanist* magazine says:

"The traditional family, with all its supposed attributes, enslaved woman; it reduced her to a breeder and caretaker of children, a servant to her spouse, a cleaning lady, and at times a victim of the labor market as well."[19]

True to the pattern of satanic doctrines, those who authored the humanistic, feminist movement promoted the rejection of God and His Word as the final authority about creation, womanhood, manhood, and marriage. Today, the proponents of feminism continue to express rejection that God's Word is to be taken literally. Furthermore, they persuade women to become dissatisfied with their God-given roles and functions in life, and they advocate the replacement of God's truths with standards and lifestyles that directly oppose the Word of God. In fact, in order to be a true disciple of the feminist philosophy a woman must directly rebel against God. This vain philosophy proposes to liberate women, but it does not; instead, it enslaves its misguided followers to Satan.

Why Christian Women Fall Prey to Feminist Philosophies

But I fear, lest by any means, as the serpent beguiled Eve through his craftiness, so your minds should be corrupted from the simplicity that is in Christ.   *II Corinthians 11:3*

Even though God has faithfully warned Christians to be vigilant against the influence and philosophies of Satan, many of our Christian contemporaries fall prey to the vain philosophy of feminism. Far too many Christian women today have been persuaded to reject the husband's role as head of the family, and they have been incited to be discontent with the honorable roles of wife, mother, and homemaker. Why have these antibiblical attitudes become an accepted part of the Christian woman's thinking?

One reason that Christian women are being deceived by this satanic doctrine is that their exposure to non-biblical opinions about feminism is proportionately greater than their exposure to biblical truths about womanhood. Virtually every American woman today is surrounded by information that is written by, or intended to appease, those who believe the philosophical viewpoint of feminism. My son and I tested this theory one day when we paid close attention to just one of the many sources of information that are intended to influence our thinking and emotions—television commercials.

The first commercial depicted a man who was unable to make a decision about whether or not to buy the services of a certain long-distance telephone company. He turned the phone over to his wife and appealed to her for leadership. A later scene showed the husband (much relieved from the responsibility of making the decision) when he learned that his wife had finalized a contract with the telephone company for its services.

The second commercial portrayed a wife who was instructing her inept husband on how to do the laundry; the next showed a wife placating her child-like husband's sweet-tooth with a healthy treat. In the fourth advertisement, a woman on a business trip was calling home to her husband and child.

All four commercials not only tried to sell their products, they also sent subtle feminist messages to unwary viewers. Three of them portrayed the husbands as child-like and inept, while the wives were knowledgeable and in control of family leadership. Even more importantly, at least three of the commercials showed the husbands in a **reversal of roles**. These husbands were shown to be functioning as their wives' **helpmates.**

Messages promoting role reversal and other tenets of feminism are not found only in advertisements, and they are not always directed at women. Nearly all of our present-day information sources send subtle messages that are meant to inform, educate, and influence the thinking of every man, woman, and child with regard to male and female roles. The majority of news reports, television programs, movies, and written materials are saturated with slanted information that is designed to influence our thinking about such real concerns as: male and female roles in marriage and society, divorce, sexual conduct, work in and out of the home, child-care, physical abuse, and sexual discrimination. In virtually every case this so-called educational material directly or indirectly opposes the biblical philosophy of womanhood and promotes the vain philosophy of feminism. The following paragraph from the *Arizona Republic* newspaper contains an example of how the message of **doubt, discontent, and disbelief** is being subtly expounded by the media.

"Even just a generation ago, most wives had **little opportunity** for infidelity. (Is the author suggesting that these women were underprivileged?) They were **stuck** (implying reluctant confinement) in their homes with their children and **other hausfraus** (name-calling is a common tactic) while their husbands went off to work, often among **attractive** co-workers." (Sowing seeds of discontent through suspicion and jealousy is also a common practice.) Emphases added.[20]

In this one paragraph alone, several subliminal notions have been implanted. Negative words and phrases such as "little opportunity," "stuck," and "hausfraus," along with other catch-words and slogans, are used for their power to influence thought and emotions. And they almost always leave the reader with negative feelings about her role as helpmate and mother. Long after a woman puts down her magazine or newspaper, these negative feelings will remain in her subconscious mind. Then, when her husband acts inconsiderately, when her child whines all day, when she feels unattractive, or when she is frustrated because "a woman's work is never done," those embedded adverse emotions can surface. Without even realizing that the source for her discontent is the unremembered exposure to this type of propaganda, a woman is likely to begin applying these negative thoughts and feelings to herself and her own circumstances. She may think to herself; "I'm stuck. I'm nothing but a frumpy housewife. I need freedom to be myself." Future twisted messages about the supposed mistreatment of women will reinforce her media-agitated emotions, causing her to feel that she **personally** is being mistreated. Unconsciously indoctrinated by misleading information, errors, false teaching, and outright lies, this woman will then dwell on and magnify the small bumps in the road of marriage that she normally would just ride over. This disastrous sequence of events, from complacency to discontent, may occur **not necessarily because of actual personal experiences,** but because of media-implanted seeds of discontent.

Countering Vain Philosophies

A woman cannot avoid being exposed to the many satanic philosophies of this world but she can counter their influence on her life. First, a biblical woman should be constantly alert to the fact that most false philosophies will appeal to her emotions, her sense of "personal rights," her desire for autonomy, and her sin-nature weaknesses. Secondly, when a woman begins to recognize the intruding influence of deceptive philosophies on her thinking, she should do as our Lord Jesus Christ did when He was confronted and tempted by Satan. Christ countered the attempt of Satan to influence His thinking and His mission in life with the absolute truth of God's Word.

> *Then saith Jesus unto him, Begone, Satan; for it is written, Thou shalt worship the Lord, thy God, and Him only shalt thou serve.*
>
> *Matthew 4:10*

It is time for Christian women to stop being influenced by satanic doctrines that oppose the truth of God's Word. However, Satan's forces are so strong in this modern world that the only sure weapon a woman has against satanic doctrines and their influence on her thinking is the mind of Christ. A woman who brings *"into captivity her every thought to the obedience of Christ"* can recognize for herself such vain philosophies as feminism, humanism, or any other ism.

> *Casting down imaginations, and every high thing that exalteth itself against the knowledge of God, and bringing into captivity every thought to the obedience of Christ.*   *II Corinthians 10:5*

God's Word contains all the philosophical knowledge that we need to live a full and satisfying life. The Bible tells us how to view ourselves in relation to God and to other people. It gives us specific rules and guidelines to follow throughout our lives, in every situation and every circumstance. It instructs us in the one and only true philosophy—God's viewpoint.

CHAPTER XIII

FAULTY THINKING PATTERNS

Vain philosophies are not the only enemy to a woman's right thinking. Her own sin nature works through her will and emotions to produce strong personal opinions that also oppose God's Word. The faulty thinking patterns that result from these opinions make living biblical womanhood almost impossible. This chapter will expose some of the types of faulty thinking patterns that are most common to women and it will suggest how such erroneous thinking can be conquered.

A woman's thinking may appear to be intelligent, logical, or even lofty, but her thoughts and opinions are formed within a very limited and imperfect human mind and so they are subject to error. By contrast, God's thoughts are infinitely unlimited and completely free of error.

> *For my thoughts are not your thoughts, neither are your ways my ways, saith the Lord. For as the heavens are higher than the earth, so are my ways higher than your ways, and my thoughts than your thoughts.* Isaiah 55:8-9

Whenever a woman hears biblical truth that is contrary to one of her previously formed opinions, she faces a critical decision. In that moment, her faulty human thinking collides with divine truth and she is forced to make a choice. Will she adhere to her own opinions, or will she switch to God's thinking? Since God's thoughts are infinitely higher than human opinions, it seems only reasonable that a Christian woman would wish to trade upward. The verse below declares that our human thinking needs to be renewed in order to understand God's will.

> *And be not conformed to this world, but be ye transformed by the renewing of your mind, that ye may prove what is that good, and acceptable, and perfect, will of God.* Romans 12:2

The following are four common examples of faulty thinking that will be compared to the Word of God. You may see yourself in one or more of these examples. Do not automatically throw off any conviction that you might feel as you work through these pages. Instead, pray for a receptive spirit so that God can reveal to you any faulty thinking pattern you might have.

Selfish Thinking

A Christian marriage counselor once said that the number one hindrance to the successful counseling of couples today is selfish thinking. A large percentage of the Christian couples who come to him for help selfishly refuse to relinquish their own personal interests in order to make their marriages work. These men and women stubbornly maintain that their own rights must come first, and they refuse the give-and-take that is necessary for two people to live in harmony. Selfish thinking exists in many Christians, even though a primary characteristic of Christianity is supposed to be a willingness to place others before oneself.

> *Let nothing be done through strife or vainglory, but in lowliness of mind let each esteem others better than themselves. Look not every man on his own things, but every man also on the things of others. Let this mind be in you, which was also in Christ Jesus.*   *Philippians 2:3-5*

The mind (attitude) which was in Christ Jesus was selflessness, manifested by His complete submission to God's will, "...*not as I will, but as thou wilt.*" *Matthew 26:39b*. Jesus did not regard Himself above God's plan nor did He place His own interests over the needs of the people He came to save. The attitude Christ had toward His designed purpose is the same attitude that Christian women should have toward living according to the principles of biblical womanhood.

Judgmental Thinking

Marriage is **the** most intimate relationship that one person can have with another. Intimacy can be the means of a comfortable and enjoyable companionship between a husband and wife, or it can be the catalyst for judgmental attitudes. As the old adage so aptly states, "familiarity breeds contempt." This familiarity results from an intimate knowledge of our mate's sin nature weaknesses, which in turn can lead to judging.

Judging is a particular problem for many women that causes them to be hypercritical of their husbands. A woman who has a problem with a judgmental thinking pattern cannot stand to leave uncorrected any perceived wrong doing. This is the ingrained mothering instinct—to correct wrong and to teach that which is right—gone wrong. The mothering instinct is necessary for training young children, but when a wife applies teaching or training to her husband it is an invasion of his privacy. The relationship between a wife and a husband was never meant to be that of mother and child. A woman should judge her own performance, but she has no right to demand perfection from her husband.

A husband's growth towards maturity can be severely hampered by a judgmental wife. His attention is drawn away from becoming aware of his need for change because his attention is focused on his wife's judgmental attitudes.

> *Let us not, therefore, judge one another any more, but judge this, rather: that no man put a stumbling block or an occasion to fall in his brother's way.*
> *Romans 14:13*

Instead of judging her husband, a woman should concentrate on bringing her own attitudes and actions up to God's expectations. A biblical woman will leave her husband in God's hands for Him to make any necessary changes.

> *In the same manner, ye wives, be in subjection to your own husbands that, if any obey not the word, they also may without the* (literally "a") *word be won by the behavior of the wives.* *I Peter 3:1*

(Note: the first occurrence of "the Word" refers to the Word of God, while the second refers to an absence of the wives' words. The Bible makes it clear that God does not need the wife as His spokesman to set her husband straight!)

Self-Righteous Thinking

A woman who indulges in judgmental thinking patterns often becomes very self-righteous as well. She is usually convinced that because she is "right," she must control the thoughts and actions of everyone around her in order to ensure their success or to prevent their failure.

As we saw in Chapter IV, the desire to control is now a strong sin-nature trait of a woman. She is often portrayed in this negative way in cartoons about women. The controlling woman is the brunt of jokes about the wife who constantly endeavors to change her husband and the mother-in-law who always interferes in her adult children's lives. Unfortunately, these jokes hit home because the self-righteous, controlling woman is so well recognized.

For the self-righteous woman, submission in marriage is extremely odious. Because she cannot trust anyone else to be right, she will fight for the decision-making position in the family. A self-righteous woman will emphasize all the faults of her husband as her excuse not to follow his leadership. If she ever does relinquish temporary leadership to her husband, it is done in teeth-gritting obedience, rather than in willing submission. The controlling woman's reluctant obedience is similar to the rebellious little girl who was **made** to sit down.

The little girl sat, but she stubbornly maintained control when she defiantly said to herself, "I'm sitting down on the outside, but I'm standing up on the inside!"

Some indications of a self-righteous woman are incessant and insistent nagging, angry arguing (especially if someone doesn't appear to accept her viewpoint), and penalizing anyone within her sphere of control who does not do what she thinks is best. Her punishments vary from pouting and cold-shoulder treatments to verbal abuse. The self-righteous woman will use any form of intimidation or other manipulation to get her own way. In order to justify her actions she will often make favorable comparisons between her sins and the supposed greater sins of other women. A controlling, self-righteous woman is very difficult to live with because she is always argumentative (contentious).

> *It is better to dwell in the wilderness, than with a contentious and an angry woman.*
>
> *Proverbs 21:19*

> *A continual dropping in a very rainy day and a contentious woman are alike.*
>
> *Proverbs 27:15*

Spiritual Superiority Thinking

One of the more insidious oppositions to biblical womanhood comes from women who know the facts of the Bible very well. These women believe that their knowledge and thus their presumed spirituality somehow enables them to live by their own rules. For instance, their faulty thinking might lead them to believe that it isn't really necessary to use corporal punishment on their rebellious children, or that they don't need to follow the leadership of their spiritually "inferior" husbands.

All of God's Word becomes subject to the private interpretation of women who presume a spiritual superiority. They may even say that the Holy Spirit has revealed something different to them, thus allowing them to bypass the revealed Word of God. Of course a biblical wife knows that the Holy Spirit never leads her to disobey God's Word.

> *Nevertheless, when he, the Spirit of truth,* (the Holy Spirit) *is come, he will guide you into all truth; for he shall not speak of himself, but whatever he shall hear, that shall he speak; and he will show you things to come. He shall glorify me* (Jesus Christ); *for he shall receive of mine, and shall show it unto you.* John 16:13-14

The woman who thinks that the Holy Spirit would give her information or insight that is in opposition to the Word of God is actually being deluded by her own human feelings or her desire for spiritual autonomy. No one can claim to have true spiritual wisdom while rejecting the Word of God and living according to her own opinions.

> *For let not that man think that he shall receive anything of the Lord. A double-minded man is unstable in all his ways.* James 1:7-8

(Note: The term "double-minded" refers to a person who thinks partially with the world's thinking, emotions, and personal opinions; and partially with God's Word.)

Oh, Wretched Woman That I Am!

This chapter has covered only four of the predominant sin-nature problems that can cause a woman to stray from biblical womanhood. We have not considered other deeds of the flesh such as hatred, jealousy, and anger *(Galatians 5:17-21)* which also can interfere with a woman's ability to live according to God's design. However, the discussion of these four problems should help you to realize that a major part of the opposition to God's design for womanhood comes from your own sin nature. When a woman recognizes the extensive influence that her sin nature can have on her thinking, she can readily identify with Paul's emotion-filled statement concerning the struggle between his sin nature and his desire to follow God's will.

> *But I see another law in my members, warring against the law of my mind, and bringing me into captivity to the law of sin which is in my members. Oh, wretched man that I am! Who shall deliver me from the body of this death?* Romans 7:23-24

If you are a woman who struggles with one or more sin-nature problems that oppose biblical womanhood (and who doesn't?), it is easy to become discouraged—but God has the solution. He has a plan for destroying the opposition and giving you victory over your sin nature.

Defeating the Opposition

The ingrained opposition to God's design for our lives can be defeated by knowledge of and adherence to the Word of God. The Christian woman has available to her the means of resisting and overcoming the unbiblical influences in her life. She does not have to be swayed by false philosophies, nor is it necessary for her to succumb to her own sin-nature tendencies. The armament that defeats such opposition is spiritual thinking.

Spiritual thinking belongs to, and comes only from, God; it comes not from anything we feel, think, or can manufacture within ourselves. Only God's Word tells us how we can obtain **His** spirituality, both for eternal salvation and for living a godly life. When a woman accepts Jesus Christ as her personal Savior she is saved for all eternity *(John 3:36);* she becomes a child of God *(John 1:12);* and she is able to have fellowship with Him in this life as well *(I John 1:9; 4:13-15).* While a woman is walking in fellowship with God, the Holy Spirit works to counter her sin nature weaknesses and produces in her the fruit of the Spirit. This is what is meant by true spirituality. The fruit of the Spirit utterly destroys any opposition to biblical womanhood.

> *But the fruit of the Spirit is love, joy, peace, longsuffering, gentleness, goodness, faith, Meekness, self-control; against such things there is no law.*   *Galatians 5:22-23*

True spirituality, as compared to the false spirituality of the one claiming to follow a private interpretation of Scripture, is manifested by the fruit of the Spirit in a believer's life.   The Holy Spirit produces in the believer only attitudes and actions that are in perfect harmony with God's laws. A woman cannot maintain true spirituality while she is living contrary to any of the written Word of God.

> *Therefore, to him that knoweth to do good, and doeth it not, to him it is sin.*   *James 4:17*

Living in opposition to God's Word is sin, and sin breaks spiritual fellowship between man and God. At that point, confession is the only prayer that restores fellowship with God.

> *If we confess our sins, He is faithful and just to forgive us our sins; and to cleanse us from all unrighteousness.*   *I John 1:9*
> *(cf Psalms 32:5; 51:1-9; Proverbs 28:13)*

An unshakeable confidence in Christ, knowledge of His Word, and walking daily in the Holy Spirit are the means by which a woman can resist the deceptive philosophies that work against the plan of God.

> *Casting down imaginations, and every high thing that exalteth itself against the knowledge of God, and bringing into captivity every thought to the obedience of Christ.*   *II Corinthians 10:5*

Every thought that is brought to *"the obedience of Christ"* destroys the opposition and leads a woman to live to the glory of God.

Living by a Truly Higher Spiritual Law

Under the law of our land today's woman is free to make decisions in opposition to her husband's leadership—"its my life, my body, my mind." God always calls a believer to do what is right spiritually above what is "right" according to current governmental law, socially accepted tradition, or popular opinion. This is following a higher spiritual law. The story of Philemon is a perfect example of a believer being asked to forgo his legal rights in favor of spiritual truth.

Philemon was a believer who was led to Christ by Paul. He had a slave named Onesimus who had run away and was therefore subject to death under the law of the land. After running away Onesimous met Paul and he also was won to Christ.

Paul wrote a letter to Philemon entreating him to treat Onesimus by the higher spiritual law. In this letter Paul acknowledged that Philemon had every **legal right** to deal harshly with his errant servant. However, Paul appealed to he higher spiritual laws of forgiveness and divine love in order to encourage Philemon to go beyond what he had the legal right to do.

Having confidence in thy obedience I wrote unto thee, knowing that thou wilt also do more than I say.　　　　　　　　　　　　　*Philemon 21*

The higher spiritual law surpasses mere compliance to laws. First, it is to know God's reason behind each law given to man, as David demonstrated in *Psalm 51:16-17*. Second, it is to act in Christian love and grace, **beyond** the letter of the law.

> It is to forgive *"seventy times seven," Matthew 18:22;* not to divorce even though you have the right, *Matthew 19:6-8;* not to sue a fellow believer even though you have been wronged, *I Corinthians 6:7;* and to set aside your own rights in order to reach your husband, *I Peter 3:1* and *I Corinthians 7:16*.

This truly higher spiritual law doesn't mean that a believer will set aside God's written Word; it means that she **willingly** submits to every law of God and, even further, sacrifices her own rights for the benefit of others. If her husband does not live according to the Word of God, she does not use that as an excuse to not live out biblical womanhood herself.

The Christian woman who consistently applies God's Word to her everyday life genuinely lives according to God's higher spiritual law. Even when her personal circumstances appear to warrant the possibility of her justifiable retaliation, she adheres to God's spiritual directions. Like the book of Philemon teaches, she goes beyond the letter of the law and doesn't demand her rights. A woman who lives according to this spiritual way of life offers love when her husband and children are unlovely, she gives when she has been rebuffed, and she does these things as a deliberate act of submission to God's will.

In Conclusion

It is not necessary for a Christian woman to fall as a casualty to vain philosophies or to succumb to her sin nature's opposition to biblical womanhood. Christ has already destroyed such enemies. As believers we can claim our victory through Him.

> *But thanks be to God, who giveth us the victory through our Lord Jesus Christ. Therefore, my beloved brethren, be ye steadfast, unmovable, always abounding in the work of the Lord, forasmuch as ye know that your labor is not in vain in the Lord.*   *I Corinthians 15:57-58*

Right now, today, simply obey the Word of God, even if you don't feel like it. Pray that God will change your mind through knowledge of His Word and that He will change your emotions through your obedience. Remember, there is power in the Word! Your trust in God will grow stronger as you obey His Word and watch Him work His miracles in your life.

I pray that each of you will realize Christ's victory over *"every high thing that exalteth itself against the knowledge of God" (II Corinthians 10:5).* As you steadfastly submit your will to God's design for biblical womanhood, I pray that you will have exceeding joy and full confidence that your *"labor is not in vain in the Lord" (I Corinthians 15:58).*

SECTION III

APPLICATIONS FOR PRACTICAL LIVING

INTRODUCTION

If you have reached this section after carefully reading through the first two sections, it indicates that you:

* Have a desire to live your life in obedience to God.

* Are willing to reevaluate your former way of thinking for possible error and to correct it where necessary.

* Are not willing for Satan to control your thinking by manipulating your emotions or sin nature.

On the other hand, if you have turned to this section out of curiosity, without having seriously studied the first two sections, you are in dangerous territory. Reading this section first is like trying to determine a recipe by looking at someone else's finished cake. Please read Sections I and II carefully before you examine the following applications of biblical womanhood.

Applications for Practical Living, sets forth mechanics for living the principles taught in Section I. This section is the "Biblical Philosophy of Womanhood and Marriage" placed into action. It gives specific how-to advice and should answer most of the questions brought to mind by Section I.

Applications for Practical Living should give you encouragement and hope that you can actually live biblical womanhood. However, you need to be aware that there are many powerful obstacles working against your success. Each woman is burdened with her own sin nature. Although she may try to live as a biblical wife, subject to her husband's rule, she still struggles with her own desire for autonomy (I want to be master of my own life). She also struggles with the fear that her husband will misuse leadership and cause her to suffer (or worse, her children to suffer). These struggles cause a modern wife to feel very vulnerable. Furthermore, the actual imperfections of her spouse creates possible stumbling blocks as she must cope with problems that are not of her own making. Finally, she must overcome the modern vain philosophies that entreat her to doubt and fear God's perfect way for marriage.

Nevertheless, obstacles to biblical womanhood can be overcome. Whether a modern Christian woman overcomes such barriers and lives as a biblical wife depends entirely on her personal commitment to God. This commitment can inspire her to search for ways to accomplish God's goal of biblical womanhood and give her the stamina to persevere, regardless of the barriers. This section will provide the committed woman many practical illustrations on how to succeed as a biblical woman in today's world.

CHAPTER XIV

DISILLUSIONS, DISAPPOINTMENTS, AND MISUNDERSTANDINGS

From the time a little girl is old enough to play house she often dreams of the day she will get married and "live happily ever after" like the princess in fairy tales. These dreams do not evaporate as a girl grows into a young woman. She continues to expect that she will someday marry a wonderful man and have a family of her own. A woman is at the height of her happiness on her wedding day because it signifies the beginning of the fulfillment of her life-long hopes and dreams. She has stardust in her eyes and her theme song is "I'll love you forever." However, in no time at all the stardust begins to seem more like fool's gold, and the theme song begins to sound like "Nobody knows the trouble I've seen." The fact is that a husband and wife can live together "happily ever after" only in fairy tales.

The unrealistic expectations of an immature girl toward marriage sets her up for major disappointments. The reality of living with a human husband soon explodes the illusions that are promoted by fairy tales. In real life, sin natures inevitably clash and the star-struck girl is forced to deal with disillusions, disappointments, and misunderstandings.

One source of disillusion for the Christian wife occurs when she knows how a Christian man is supposed to treat his wife, that is to love her *"even as Christ also loved the church. . ." (Ephesians 5:25).* A woman who understands what is perfect and right for a biblical marriage may reasonably expect it to be that way. When it is not, she can feel cheated and disappointed. In order to deal with life as it really is she must not forget that although God's ways are perfect, the people who attempt to live His ways are decidedly imperfect.

A wife's disappointments in marriage can be because of her unrealistic expectations, or because even her reasonable expectations are not being met. In either case her disappointments will remain unresolved unless she faces her marriage realistically. No wife can expect to have a trouble-free marriage. Marriage is not a fairy tale or the union of two perfect people. It is two imperfect people, one of whom is a husband who causes his wife some very real problems. The most practical first step to resolving problems with a husband is to understand the make-up of the man.

Understanding Your Husband

In order for a wife to live with her husband in a practical manner, she must make every effort to understand her man as he really is. Chapters VII, VIII, and the following will help a woman to better understand the man who is her husband.

Many disappointments a wife faces in marriage are simply because of the differences between the drives (other than sexual) of men and women. Most women are very relationship oriented. Courtship days are probably one of the happiest times of a woman's life, because she and her future husband spend a great deal of time together. During this time a woman's future husband becomes the center of her life. She usually assumes that her fiancee wants to make her the center of his life as well. Therefore, when after the wedding her husband's pursuit ceases somewhat, or even altogether, she may become confused and hurt. Because he no longer does the things he did while they dated, she may begin to feel that her husband doesn't love her anymore. A wife can overcome many of her disappointments when she accepts that her husband's drives in their relationship are not, nor ever will be, identical to her own.

In contrast to a woman's desire to make her man the center of her life, a man's major drive is to lead, protect, and provide for his family (Chapter VII). However, such responsibility is an extremely difficult, lonely, and discouraging task. Therefore, a man's goal during courtship is to identify and to secure a supportive helpmate and companion. He feels a strong need for a wife to ease his loneliness and to support his responsibility. A man is attracted to the woman who supports his dreams for the future and the one who encourages him during the times he feels like giving up.

Once a man has married, the objective of winning the woman of his choice is completed and the husband is ready to move on to conquer his main pursuits—that of protecting and providing for his family. Furthermore, he expects his wife to move on to become his helpmate—that is to help make his task less lonely and difficult. He too, may feel puzzled when he discovers that his wife wants to continue the activities of courtship, rather than to move on to other goals of living. This fact may not be very flattering to a woman's romantic, feminine soul, but men are motivated more by goals than by their emotions. It isn't that a man is totally void of any emotional desire for intimacy, however developing close relationships is not usually a goal a man actively works to achieve.

Problem-Solving Through Communication

Looking objectively at a problem and searching for principles that are in keeping with God's design for manhood and womanhood are very important steps in problem-solving. But, simply understanding does not always eliminate a woman's disappointments. She may still feel like something is missing in her marriage and she may have some emotional needs that she wants her husband to fulfill. Communication is also an essential step for resolving problems and attaining intimacy in marriage.

It can be a very emotional experience for a woman to talk about her unfulfilled needs. It must be remembered, however, that a woman will not properly communicate to an objective man when she is highly emotional. A man has a tendency to discount the importance of a woman's words when she is emotionally charged, or he may tune her out altogether. For a woman to communicate with a man, she must speak in a language that penetrates his masculine thinking pattern. The following basic steps will help prepare you for meaningful communication with your husband.

Before you attempt to communicate with your husband about marriage problems, you need to prepare yourself mentally and spiritually.

* **Examine and judge** your own life. Condemning another, even when they are wrong, does not make you right *(Matthew 7:1-5; II Corinthians 10:12)*. The questions to ask yourself are "Am I living my life according to the biblical teaching for wives? Am I serving as a true helpmate, honoring my husband's leadership and supporting his manhood?"

* **Be spiritually prepared**. Ask yourself, "Is God and His Word first in my life and am I walking in fellowship with Him?" Make sure you are walking in fellowship with God and, therefore, are able to approach your husband with an attitude of submission.

* **Pray** for God to prepare your husband's heart and to quiet your emotions so that you may have a constructive discussion.

Communicating With Your Husband

After you have prepared **yourself** spiritually you are ready to approach your husband with your problem.

* **Be considerate**. Choose your timing carefully. Do not try to talk to your husband when he is especially tired,

worried, sick, or the minute he enters the door after work. Wait until he is relaxed and in a good mood.

* **Prepare your husband for discussion**. For instance, you may ask your husband to set aside time to talk about a problem you are having. If he seems reluctant to talk at the exact moment that you have chosen, ask him to let you know when he will be able to talk with you. Be sure to tell your husband that your request is very important to you.

* **Present your needs rather than throw accusations.** For instance, presenting needs could include, "I miss the talks we used to have. I really feel lonely and I need to be more a part of your life." Accusations would include, "You never talk to me anymore. You have shut me out of your life because you're insensitive."

Please, notice the objective "I need" that comes across in the first example and the accusing "You bad boy" in the second. Your husband will most likely respond positively to a request, but he will definitely bristle and defend himself if he feels like a bad little boy who is in trouble with mommy.

* **Help your husband fulfill your requests by giving him suggestions that are goal-oriented.** For instance, ask him if you could make it a practice to go out on a weekly date, or ask if he could turn off the TV for an hour occasionally just to talk. Perhaps, you would like an evening walk, or _____ you fill in the

blank with whatever would help provide the warmth that you need in your marriage. Again, this method gives your husband an objective goal he can accomplish, rather than confronts him with a challenge that may make him feel like ignoring you or putting you down.

* **Listen as well as talk.** The doors of communication go two ways, so be ready to listen and be willing to make some changes yourself. You may find that when you talk to your husband about your unfulfilled needs, he has a complaint or two of his own. He may tell you that he doesn't talk to you because you don't give him time to unwind when he gets home from work. Your husband may reveal that you frequently interrupt him, or perhaps that you change the subject to your own interests and go on and on about details that are interesting only to yourself. There are many things your husband may tell you that will bring you closer together when you open the doors for two-way communication.

Giving Communication Time

After a woman has communicated a problem to her husband she usually expects some immediate changes to take place. However, this does not always occur. If your husband does slip back into his old ways and forgets the plan that you both agreed upon, it's all right to remind him. However, approach him in the same manner and with the same guidelines as before. Avoid resorting to techniques of nagging, belittling, or shaming him in order to get your own way; and **never** compare his actions with how other men treat their wives. You might begin your conversation with "Honey, did you change your mind about doing _____ with me?"

Habits are hard to change. It has been said that it takes at least thirty tries to change a habit. Give your husband time to accomplish what you are asking of him. Also, pay close attention and show your appreciation when he deliberately does what you want, such as turning off the TV to talk. Your appreciation will demonstrate that you don't have merely a desire to control, but that your needs are real. If you do not notice his attempts to please you, or if you only point out when he slips up, he will probably quit trying altogether.

When Things Don't Improve

In every marriage a wife must accept that there are some things about her husband that will never change—at least not for a very long time. In such cases constant reminders tend only to sound like chronic complaining and usually avail nothing. A wife's attitude toward unchanging irritations should be an attitude of acceptance and forgiveness, just as the Lord has accepted and forgiven her.

> *Put on, therefore, as the elect of God, holy and beloved, tender mercies, kindness, humbleness of mind, meekness, longsuffering; Forbearing one another, and forgiving one another, if any man have a quarrel against any; even as Christ forgave you, so also do ye.* Colossians 3:12-13

156

At the beginning of this chapter we spoke of fairy tales. In fairy tales the frog turns into a charming prince. In real life, the prince sometimes becomes a frog who gets mud on the carpet and embarrasses his wife in public. The truth is that living according to biblical principles for womanhood means living with the frog, as well as with the prince. Sometimes putting biblical principles into action means that a wife must deal with her less-than-charming husband while he acts immaturely, and she must continue to follow his leadership even while he is not walking with God. Furthermore, she will suffer along side him during the unpleasant consequences of his immaturity and sin. A biblical wife will honor her husband's position of authority, even if it takes fifty years for him to allow God to break that immaturity. Sometimes, I think that modern women would better comprehend the reality of their marriage vows if the wedding ceremony included:

> "I promise to trust God while my husband grows up. I will learn to understand his masculine characteristics. I will remain respectful even when I think he is acting immaturely. I will share the consequences of all his mistakes and I will persevere through all disillusions, disappointments, and misunderstandings, till death do us part."

As it is, most brides today believe that marriage is a 50/50 relationship and they promise to "love, honor, and obey," without the slightest hint of what they are really getting into. The biblical principle for marriage is not a 50/50 contractual arrangement. Instead, it is a 100% commitment on each individual's part. Although it is **easiest** when the other mate

157

does his or her part, each person is still responsible for giving his or her 100% commitment. A Christian wife should operate within her role as a helpmate even when her husband does not always respond to her needs. In the end, it is not what another person does that commends us; but commendation comes to those who simply do what is right, without expectations of any immediate reward.

> *And let us not be weary in well doing; for in due season we shall reap, if we faint not. As we have, therefore, opportunity, let us do good unto all men, especially unto them who are of the household of faith.* Galatians 6:9-10

CHAPTER XV

IRRITATIONS, FRUSTRATIONS, AND AGGRAVATIONS

If you have a typical marriage, your husband probably has at least one habit that drives you insane. The bathroom is left like a gorilla just showered and shaved. He eats a certain messy or disgusting way, he puts his dirty socks on the coffee table, or _____ you fill in the blank. You and your husband will have a blend of your very own irritants.

A wife can nag her gorilla about how he left the bathroom, she can throw his socks at him, or as we saw in the last chapter she can learn to solve problems through objective communication. Communication is always the best way to deal with the problems that occur in a marriage. However, proper communication between a husband and a wife is sometimes difficult to achieve. Just as the different drives of men and women can pave the way for disappointments and misunderstandings, their different way of thinking can make communication extremely difficult. These differences cause mis-communication, which is probably the major hindrance to the resolution of problems in marriage.

Let's look at three examples of how poor communication can separate a husband and a wife and how it can prevent them from resolving their problems. Following each example we will see how a wife can simultaneously use objective communication principles, find a solution to her problem, and be a biblical helpmate to her husband.

Example One, What's Wrong With This Picture?

John has a habit of coming home each evening and immediately sitting down to read his newspaper. Mary is tired of this routine and on this particular evening she glares at the back of the newspaper, sighs, and goes into the kitchen slamming the door behind her. After about ten minutes, John becomes aware that there is a lot of noise going on in the kitchen. He can hear Mary muttering as she roughly tosses pots and pans onto the stove and slams the refrigerator door. John calls out, "What's wrong with you?" to which Mary replies, "If you loved me, you'd know what's wrong."

What's wrong with this picture is that Mary is holding John responsible for understanding something that he is not built to understand. John may love his wife very much, but love alone does not help him decode Mary's words and actions. In this case it is up to Mary to communicate objectively to John what her problem is and how he can help her solve it.

Let's Correct This Picture

First, Mary should evaluate what it is that is making her feel so frustrated. For instance, her thoughts may be, "John never talks to me anymore." Next, she should present her need to John. This part is tricky. Remember, a woman's thoughts are never far removed from her emotions, but her emotions do not communicate well to a man's objective mind. For instance, "John **never** talks to me anymore," is a statement of Mary's emotional reaction to the **feeling** of being shut out, rather than a clear declaration of what is actually true. If Mary presents only her feelings to John, then she will communicate something entirely different than what she means to say. John will most likely take her emotional words literally and his first reaction will be, "That's ridiculous, of course I talk to you. I asked you what was wrong, and I'm talking to you **now** aren't I?"

In order to communicate properly, Mary needs to translate her feelings into the objective words that will accurately acquaint John with her real need—in this case she needs conversation. The translation from female language (a language of feelings) to male language (a literal language) is necessary before John can provide what Mary truly wants. Mary might say "John, after you've rested for a while, I need to talk to you." Then, when John is ready to talk, Mary could say, "Lately, I've been feeling lonely. I've evaluated why I'm feeling this way and I realized it's because we aren't talking like we used to. I really need for us to set aside time each day, just for conversation."

God's Word instructs a husband to provide for his wife's needs in a loving and understanding way. Most husbands would be quite happy to provide what their wives need—**if** they could just understand what that is. A wife is functioning as a biblical helpmate when she helps her husband understand how to fulfill his role as a loving husband. In most cases, all a wife must do is to respect her husband's objectivity and translate her feelings into concrete goals that he can both understand and successfully accomplish. If a woman is willing to learn this translation technique, she will be in a better position to achieve the closeness that both she and her husband desire.

Example Two, The Case of the Unconscious Husband

There are many irritations and aggravations that can occur simply because a woman has standards for housekeeping and a man is oblivious to those standards. For instance, I know one woman whose husband would invariably wash his hands in the kitchen just after she left a colander of lettuce draining in the sink. It drove her crazy when he absentmindedly rinsed the soap from his hands right on top of her lettuce. This wife repeatedly complained to her husband, but to no avail. Finally, she realized that part of the problem was that her husband wasn't aware of the lettuce in the sink at all. When she said "Don't wash your hands there!," she didn't fully communicate. Since she never mentioned the lettuce, her literal husband thought that his wife objected to him **ever** washing his hands in the kitchen. He considered his wife's complaints totally unreasonable.

Finally, the woman in our illustration realized that the way she worded her problem caused her husband to feel under personal attack. Her solution was to make her complaint impersonal by drawing her husband's attention to the inanimate lettuce. She began to say, "Honey, let's remove the lettuce before you wash your hands." It only took a few repetitions before her husband became alert to the real problem, and now he removes the lettuce from the sink without reminders. This approach not only eliminates a great deal of irritation, it also saves a lot of lettuce.

Example Three, The Unsolvable Problem

There are some annoying habits that a husband will never change. For instance, the husband in our above illustration has a habit of shaking his freshly-washed hands before drying them. Now, when this man does something he does it with vigor, so water is splattered everywhere when he shakes his hands (a little like a wet dog). No matter how his wife has worded her problem, this husband's habit went unchanged for more than thirty years.

When a woman must live with small irritations that never seem to change, they can begin to grow in her mind until they become mountainous frustrations. The wife in our illustration realized that her frustration level was growing far out of proportion to the seriousness of the crime. This wife knew that the only solution in this case was to change her own attitude, rather than to expect her husband to change his habit. First, she reminded herself that when her husband goes on trips, her dry counter tops become lonely reminders that he is away. When he is gone for a very long time, she misses his presence so much that she would gladly clean up water just to have him home. Why not maintain that same positive attitude when he isn't away but is at home splattering mirrors? After all, how important is a little water compared to the love, provision, protection, and companionship that he so freely gives to her? By modifying her own attitude, this wife now smiles while she cleans mirrors and counter tops. She can even laugh about and enjoy her husband's eccentricities. Sometimes a simple decision to look at problems in a more positive manner can eliminate frustration and elicit appreciation instead.

A wife is to be her husband's helper on earth, which includes helping him to be aware of her needs. But it is not her job as a helpmate to force changes. A wife's love and acceptance may eventually produce in her husband a desire to make positive changes, but angry demands will only draw out his stubborn streak and seriously hinder any positive change. However, here's a word of hope. An interesting phenomena often occurs when a wife accepts her husband as he is—he changes on his own. It's as if the husband is tuning out what sounds to him like nagging, but once he feels fully accepted by his wife he makes a special effort to please her. This happened for me. After years of complaining about soap on my lettuce, my husband cooperated within two days—once I changed my attitude. And, after more than thirty years of marriage, my husband is now drying the counter tops and mirrors after he washes and shaves. Changing your own attitude can produce miraculous rewards—in time.

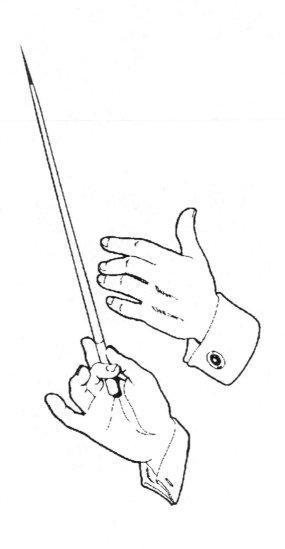

CHAPTER XVI

SUPPORTING YOUR HUSBAND'S LEADERSHIP

Leadership being a male responsibility was ordained by God, not created by sinful men with a hunger for power, as feminist claim. The husband's role can be traced back to the garden, long before sin tainted Adam and Eve *(I Corinthians 11:3, 7-9; Ephesians 5:31* compared with *Genesis 2:24* and *I Timothy 2:12-14).*

Although sin diminished Adam's ability to lead perfectly, his responsibility to God for leading Eve remained intact. The first indication after the fall that sin had not shifted this responsibility is illustrated in *Genesis 3:9* when God asked Adam, *"Where art thou?"* Eve had sinned first, but God did not seek her out first. He called to Adam because the man was in the leadership position. Adam's sin was twofold. Not only did he eat of the forbidden fruit, but he followed Eve's directions rather than fulfill his responsibility of leadership *(Genesis 3:17a).*

Throughout the Old Testament, husbands were clearly responsible to God for the leadership of their families. The accounts of Noah, Abraham, Isaac, Jacob, and others illustrate this well. The Bible tells of many events where sin corrupted these husbands' leadership, but that did not change their God-appointed roles. Today, husbands continue to be responsible for the leadership of their wives as evidenced by the verses already referenced above, as well as *I Timothy 3:4-5.*

Many Christian women intellectually accept the biblical evidence that the husband is responsible for leadership, but they still have a problem putting their knowledge into practice. Sin has further corrupted a woman's willingness to follow, just as it has corrupted a man's proficiency for leading well. This chapter will discuss some of the skills a wife needs in order to obey God and follow her all-too-human husband. We will deal with three types of real-life husbands that a wife might have. The first example deals with a husband who has little desire to lead his family at all. This is the passive or non-leader type of husband. The second example discusses the husband who is overbearing in his leadership. He will be called the aggressive husband. The third example concerns a Christian woman's fear of following an unspiritual husband. The unspiritual husband can either be an unbeliever or a believer who is not committed in his personal relationship with God.

As you read this chapter keep in mind that few men are always passive, always aggressive, or always out of touch with God. A real-life husband's leadership will vary somewhere between these extremes. His leadership may also fluctuate from time to time and from issue to issue. For instance, a husband may be an excellent father, but exercise domineering control over his wife's life as if she were a child too. Or, he may be a great provider, but be completely indifferent to his role as spiritual leader of his family. Because each husband is a unique mixture of his own sin nature traits, his upbringing, and his personal development, it is not possible to cover the precise leadership problem that a wife might face in her marriage. However, the three problem areas mentioned above will be discussed along with solutions on how a wife can be an effective helpmate, even under the most extreme types of leadership. You will then need to discern which principles are to be utilized with your husband. You will discover that the information presented can easily be mixed and matched to your particular man.

Type One, The Passive Husband

Many husbands today tend to be passive in their leadership. Male passivity is often a result of incorrect child-training or painful experiences that have severely damaged the man's ego. A man who possesses a damaged male ego is insecure about his leadership ability. However, with time and patience a biblical wife can nurse her husband's ailing ego and encourage him to overcome this insecurity. A biblical helpmate will encourage her husband in his proper masculine role without mothering him (trying to prevent bad things from happening), teaching him, or taking over his leadership responsibilities.

Passive men are usually afraid of the responsibility of leadership. They will typically procrastinate in making decisions, hoping time will make a decision unnecessary, or hoping someone else will make the decision and take the responsibility from them. These men actually prefer to share leadership responsibilities with their wives. The frustration that wives of passive husbands feel often prompts them to just take over the leadership role and make most of the family decisions themselves. These wives take over because they believe nothing will be done if they do not do it themselves. Unfortunately, the wife who takes over encourages her husband's lack of leadership and relieves him of his responsibility. For instance, a wife who is concerned about her husband's poor decisions concerning money only makes it easier for her husband to remain irresponsible when she takes over the family budget. While she is trying to prevent short-ranged bad things from happening (like a poor credit record) her husband is being prevented from facing the reality of consequences for poor judgment. If he had to deal with the consequences of his overspending, he might in time learn from the experience. But, his wife's control aborts this type of learning experience, and therefore he will probably keep over-spending (sometimes on the sly to keep "mommy" from knowing).

The following guidelines of what a biblical wife **can** do will help clarify how to be the best helpmate to a passive husband.

1. Pray fervently that God will cause your husband to become alert to his leadership responsibilities. Pray for your own strength to endure with grace the consequences of your husband's lack of leadership.

2. "Minor" in your husband's bad points. Nothing tears down a man's ego like constant criticism. Repetitive criticism tells your husband that he doesn't measure up to your standards for manhood. This only results in making a passive man weaker.

3. Respectfully ask for your husband's leadership. Ask him for his insight, **even on decisions that you could make yourself.** Then, do things his way. If he wants you to pay the bills because he hates the detail of writing checks, addressing envelopes, etc., do it. But, ask him to decide when and how much to pay.

Be sure to tell your husband how much you appreciate his insight whenever he gives you good advice. However, should his advice fail, do not make a big deal out of it; simply ask him how to fix the problem. Never say "I told you so" when things go wrong. Fear of your reaction to his mistakes will only cause your husband to further withdraw his leadership.

4. Most passive husbands are hesitant to take a firm stand on anything, and they usually cannot respond quickly to requests for advice. Therefore, present your need for a leadership decision, and then offer to wait for the answer after his consideration. Patiently leave the decision in your husband's hands. It is a wife's responsibility to let her husband know the date that a decision must be made and the cost for missing that date—**once.** Yes, watch things go undone, if necessary. If he later asks why something has gone undone, simply explain you are waiting for his decision on the matter. Remember, the take-over-wife may solve today's problem with her constant reminders, but she promotes her husband's inactive leadership and her short-sighted impatience assures hundreds of future problems.

5. If your husband specifically asks you to do something for him, do it immediately. When a passive husband asks for something, even if it's a timid hint, that **is** his leadership. Don't insist that he spell out every detail and issue a direct order. Be ready to please and willing to follow even his indirect attempts at leadership. You can always respectfully ask, "Are you suggesting that I do____?" Or, "When would you like for me to do that?"

6. It is imperative for a passive husband to have a wife who does not debate or critique his every decision. Treating his timid decisions as if he might be making some kind of horrible mistake will only defeat your goal of building up your husband. If you must ask questions about his decision in order to clarify what is expected of you, do so with a respectful attitude and a willingness to follow.

7. Give him room. It takes time to make positive changes in anyone's life. A passive husband needs a wife who accepts him as he is **before** he will have the courage to improve. This can take a long time. In the meantime, "minor" in his shortcomings and "major" in his good points.

8. "Major" in your husband's good points. Make a list of all your husband's good points and practice showing him appreciation in those areas. There is no better medicine for building up a passive husband than honest praise for who and what he is already.

I am not suggesting that a wife should ever use dishonest flattery or manipulative techniques. The goal behind honest praise is for the benefit of another, but the goal of flattery is to get something for yourself. Biblical praise and appreciation encourages a man for his accomplishments, while manipulative techniques promote weakness. The following is an illustration of how manipulative techniques will promote weakness in the man who gives in to them.

> A certain wife did not like her husband's relatives and wanted to spend every holiday exclusively with her own family. After several years of neglecting his family, the husband began to feel guilty. However, every time he tried to discuss the issue with his wife she would say, "Let's not discuss that now." Then, she would initiate sex and tell her husband what a wonderful lover he was. This wife's manipulative technique was subconsciously understood by her husband, and he was aware that he was exchanging his leadership role for momentary pleasure, but he acquiesced anyway. As a result he saw himself as a weak man who could be easily controlled by the flesh, and he disrespected his wife for using him.

By contrast, a biblical wife's honest words of praise will not result in weakening her husband's opinion of her or of himself.

Type Two, The Aggressive Husband

The aggressive husband can be described as opinionated, demanding, and domineering. Believe it or not, the aggressive man is just as insecure as is the passive one. In order to cover up feelings of inadequacy the passive man retreats while the aggressive man attacks. Both men have egos that have been damaged or untrained, and both need the help of their wives in order to heal from that damage. Therefore, a biblical wife should treat her aggressive husband's ego with the same tender care she would offer to a passive husband. Honest praise and appreciation for his good points is just as important for the aggressive husband as it is for the passive one. In addition to honest praise and appreciation, a wife can take the following steps in order to help her aggressive husband learn that his intimidation is not necessary.

1. Pray that God will cause your husband to become aware of the need for consideration for how others may feel. Pray for your own strength and spiritual wisdom in dealing with your husband.

2. Trust God for emotional protection for both you and your children.

3. Treat your husband with all the understanding, kindness, and forgiveness that you possibly can give.

Put on, therefore, as the elect of God, holy and beloved, tender mercies, kindness, humbleness of mind, meekness, longsuffering; Forbearing one another, and forgiving one another, if any man have a quarrel against any; even as Christ forgave you, so also do ye.

Colossians 3:12-13

4. Be willingly submissive. Never speak to your husband in an attacking manner and never back him into a corner with attacks on his manhood. A soft reply defuses unfair or angry demands much faster than does retaliation or a refusal to comply.

A soft answer turneth away wrath, but grievous words stir up anger. *Proverbs 15:1*

5. Ask your husband if there is anything you can do to help him. Most likely you are not the reason your husband has developed an intimidating personality, but be prepared to consider that your actions might be compounding a problem that already exists. Have you been argumentative, debated his every decision, rejected his leadership, or been unappreciative of what he has done well? Have you challenged his manhood? (Review, Chapters V through IX.) Be willing to make changes in yourself where necessary.

6. Very often a man's aggressiveness is an act of self-protection. Such a man is usually unable to trust that other people do not intend to cause him emotional pain. Therefore, it is important for a wife to earn her husband's trust by showing him that his best interest is the reason for all she says or does. A wife who gets into the habit of angry verbal attacks, snide remarks, or cutting put-downs, will never gain her husband's trust. Difficult as it is to pet a porcupine, you can get one to roll over and allow you to stroke its stomach **after** you have gained its trust. Although it is very

difficult to hold our own tongue while another person is verbally attacking us, it can be done. If a wife wishes to help her aggressive husband she must refrain from becoming aggressive herself.

He that is slow to wrath is of great understanding,
but he that is hasty of spirit exalteth folly.
Proverbs 14:29

7. Important! Calmly tell your husband that his harsh words or actions hurt you. Help him understand that you want to be his helpmate and that a more gentle request is all that is necessary. Before you talk to your husband, however, be sure your attitude is not defensive or attacking. Do not condemn him, but do let him know how much his aggression hurts you.

Type Three, The Unspiritual Husband

There are two types of unspiritual husbands—the one who is unsaved, and the one who **is** saved but is not committed to living the Christian way of life. A Christian wife should treat her unspiritual husband with the same respectful and submissive attitude as she would the most spiritual Christian husband, plus:

1. Pray for God to reveal his need for salvation or commitment to live for God. Do not nag him, constantly tell him he is a sinner, or treat him as a second-class person. Pray that you won't fall into pride's trap of feeling superior to your husband.

2. Teach your children to respect and obey their father. **Do not** undermine the children's respect by implying that he is of lesser value because he is unspiritual. In fact, it is best if they do not know, at least not until they are old enough to handle the knowledge without judgment or feelings of superiority. The admonition of *I Peter* is the same for wives of unbelieving husbands as it is for wives of uncommitted Christian husbands.

In the same manner, ye wives, be in subjection to your own husbands that if any obey not the word, they also may without the (literally "a") *word be won by the behavior of the wives, while they behold your chaste conduct coupled with fear.*

I Peter 3:1-2

3. Put yourself in God's hands and be prepared for pressure to come into your husband's life. When you pray for God to reveal to your husband his need for salvation (or his need for a committed Christian life) and when you are openly operating as a biblical wife, God will be working to catch your husband's attention. Pressures may come to bear that are intended by God to prepare your husband to be receptive to the Word of God. (Loss of job, illness, and accidents all have been used to bring tough guys to their knees.) This time period will be critical for both you and your husband. A loving and supportive biblical wife is perhaps even more important at this time than at any other. You must be willing to endure the pressures that God intends to use as a means to turn your

179

husband to Him. You must endure while you also refrain from attempting to remove those pressures. If you try to protect your husband from experiencing pressure, you will be interfering with God's purposes for that pressure. However, if you do endure, your loyalty will form a bond that can be the basis for your renewed relationship with your husband.

4. Be diligent about your own spiritual life. Study the Word of God and apply the principles within it. Go to a church where you will be saturated with the teaching of the Word of God. **However,** here comes the tough one: some husbands say that they do not want their wives to attend church. If your husband tells you not to go to church, **do not go**. If he only knows one verse of the Bible, it will be the one about wives submitting to their husbands.

There are many ways of receiving Bible teaching and Christian fellowship with other women in the interim without going to church. Day-time classes, books, personal Bible reading, tapes, and the friendship of other believing women, can carry you for a while. Yes, church is the best place to learn the Word, have fellowship, and exercise your spiritual gift, but first things first. Remember, God wants you in church even more than you want it. Give Him a chance to arrange it His way, while perhaps winning your husband at the same time.

My husband was once on a radio talk show and mentioned the concept of submitting to a husband, even by not going to church if necessary. Two ladies called the show and testified that God answered their prayers in exactly this manner. One lady testified that she was at first fearful that she would never be able to go to church, but she decided to pray, be a biblical wife, and trust God. Within a year her husband was so impressed with her submissive attitude that he not only let her go to church, but attended with her. Her husband was "won" by the behavior of his *I Peter 3* wife when he soon accepted Christ as his Saviour.

I believe that most husbands will not keep their wives from attending church, at least not for very long. Those husbands who do so are usually the ones whose wives have used their religion as a weapon. Such a wife uses the Bible to condemn her husband, and yet, rarely adheres to biblical principles herself by being the best possible helpmate. Her husband invariably believes that his wife's actions are condoned by the Bible or the church, and therefore, he wants nothing to do with Christianity. Non-submissive, religious nagging will seriously limit the possibility of a wife being God's instrument to win her husband to Christ, and her lack of grace serves only to prolong her own agony. Caution: Never, never discuss what you perceive as your husbands problems with other people—even for the purpose of prayer. Always protect your husbands dignity and right to privacy.

In Conclusion

Just as most women today do not begin marriage as mature helpmates, few men enter marriage as accomplished leaders. Furthermore, every husband has at least one area of life where he lacks maturity. A biblical wife must develop a long-ranged objective viewpoint toward her husband. She needs to look for solutions to problems that will be beneficial to them both in the long run. She should avoid the temptation of solutions that only patch things up for her own temporary comfort.

A biblical wife does not need to think that she should fix all problems that her husband may have. Her husband's shortcomings are in capable hands when they are left for God to deal with in His good time. A wife can pray about her husband's problems, but she must understand that she is not her husband's conscience, his new mother, or his spiritual mentor. She can discuss and make suggestions, but she should not attempt to protect her husband from the natural consequences of his immaturity. A wife can help with the implementation of a plan, but it is not her mission to remove her husband's responsibility of leadership by controlling all details of the plan. A woman is responsible, however, to tend to her own areas of immaturity and to allow God to develop the biblical characteristics that will enable her to be an effective helpmate. Sometimes, God even uses an imperfect husband as the means to develop a woman's maturity and biblical virtues.

Perhaps the most important virtue any wife can possess is a loving attitude that radiates a willingness to sacrifice her personal interests for her husband's best interest. A loving attitude will help her to speak honestly, but kindly, even while discussing touchy subjects. It will cause her to look for ways to build up her husband, and it will cause her to refrain from ever deliberately putting him down for his shortcomings. A loving attitude will prevent a wife from retaliating when telling her husband how he has hurt her. It will cause her to be diligent in her own spiritual life, to pray fervently for all those whom she loves, and to depend entirely on the grace of God for the outcome.

Biblical truth will get a wife through any circumstance that can occur with a real-life husband, simply because her hope is rooted in her omnipotent God. God's omnipotence parted the sea for Moses and His power can steer any passive, aggressive, disobedient, or unbelieving husband. How God chooses to move a husband, however, is rarely as dramatic as the parting of the sea. More often, He uses a biblical wife who remains submissive and empathetic, even when her husband is not all he should be. A biblical wife can believe God's Word, just as Moses did. When she possesses biblical characteristics and faithfully acts upon God's principles for womanhood, she can expect that in God's good time she will walk dry-shod across her own sea.

CHAPTER XVII

SUPPORTING YOUR HUSBAND'S ROLE AS PROVIDER AND PROTECTOR

When a business leader has the help of a competent and cooperative staff, he is able to increase his effectiveness many times over. In the same way the quality of a helpmate's influence makes a positive impact on her husband's success as leader, provider, and protector. In the preceding chapters, we discovered the impact of a wife's influence on her husband's leadership. This chapter will discuss how a wife can influence her husband's responsibility as provider and protector.

The Biblical Model

From the very beginning of time God made it clear that men were to protect and provide for their wives. Men were to till the soil, to be drafted and fight the wars, and to take care of their own families. In fact, in the New Testament a man who provided *"not for his own, and specially for those of his own house, he hath denied the faith, and is worse than an infidel"* (I Timothy 5:8).

A husband's responsibilities as provider and protector are also derived from Scripture references that portray God as like a husband to believers. In *Deuteronomy 10:18* God speaks of Himself as a husband to Israel who executes justice (protection) for the fatherless and widow and who gives the stranger nourishment (provision). The New Testament refers to Christ as the husband of the church in *II Corinthians 11:2* and *Revelation 21:2 & 9*. The model for how a human husband is to lead, provide, and protect is Christ.

> *For the husband is the head of the wife, even as Christ is the head of the church; and He is the savior of the body . . . Husbands; love your wives, even as Christ also loved the church, and gave Himself for it.*　　　　*Ephesians 5:23 & 25*

A husband's responsibility for protecting and providing for a wife and family gives balance to his leadership authority. A man may be the master of his castle, but his sense of protectiveness tempers the power of his authority. For this reason it is to a woman's distinct advantage to support and encourage her husband's manhood in the areas of provision and protection.

Supporting Your Husband's Role As Provider

Inherent within a man is an awareness that he alone bears the ultimate responsibility to support his wife and family. Because even very masculine or well-trained men are secretly fearful that they will not be able to live up to this responsibility of manhood, they are very vulnerable to feelings of failure if their wives do not appreciate their efforts. When a wife appreciates her husband's provisional efforts she helps bolster his manly confidence. Her support comforts him while he works under difficult bosses, gives him courage when he faces competitive fellow employees, and eases the fatigue of long, hard hours at a job he may even dislike. The following are some specific ways a helpmate can encourage her husband in his effort to provide for his family.

1. **Do**—help make his home a retreat from the rigors of the workplace. Ask your husband how you can make your home special for him. He may ask for a special chair that no one else uses, or perhaps a special spot to spread out his hobby. No matter how large or how small your home is, make it a place where he can gather strength in order to recover from the hardships of his workplace. A home can be a husband's castle as well as a wife's nest to feather.

2. **Do**—find out what your husband needs in order to unwind after work. I once knew a husband who asked only for a glass of iced tea and thirty quiet minutes with the paper before dinner. This request unbelievably became a major contention between the couple. The wife said that her days were too busy with the children for her to remember to have tea ready the minute he got home. She complained that the children were too hungry to wait for dinner and that he was thinking only of himself; therefore, she dismissed his request as selfish and unreasonable. This husband interpreted his wife's attitude to mean that she considered his needs trivial and bothersome. Tragically, he later found another woman who was more sensitive to his needs.

I am not suggesting that this marriage ended because the husband did not get his glass of tea. The wife's resistance to preparing tea was merely an overt symptom of her underlying poor attitude. Her negative attitude toward her husband's wishes permeated everything she did and said. Nor am I excusing the husband for his adultery. He was as deficient a leader as she was a helpmate. I am only pointing out the significant role that this wife played in the break-up of her own marriage.

3. **Do**—sympathetically listen to your husband's work difficulties and be a sounding board as he talks out possible solutions for his problems. **Beware**, however, that a husband does not need for his wife to take over and try to solve all his dilemmas. A biblical helpmate encourages her husband to persevere **through** his troubles; a take-over wife tries to help him escape **from** his responsibilities. Usually, all a husband needs is a sympathetic ear and a helpmate to stand by him in his final decision. In this way she is encouraging him to fulfill his leadership responsibilities.

4. **Do**—carefully manage the household within your husband's income. The money a husband receives for his labor represents the sacrifice of many hours of his personal life; it is, therefore, a portion of himself. A wife's proper handling of her husband's money is proportional to the respect she has for him personally and for his life-sacrifice.

A wife needs to be very careful about how she treats her husband's provisions. Even seemingly innocent remarks, such as apologizing to visitors for the cheapness of their furniture, can cause a husband to feel like a failure as a provider. A wife who constantly complains that her husband does not provide enough, or squanders that which he does provide, defeats her husband's resolve to provide. A wife who nags for extra luxuries that are beyond her husband's ability to give is also telling him that he is deficient as a provider.

On the other hand, a wife who learns to be an expert at money-management helps her husband provide for his family successfully. Her loving care for their possessions and her appreciation for his hard work, no matter how much or how little he earns, gives his ambition a boost and encourages his resolve to provide.

Supporting Your Husband's Role As Protector

For thousands of years men have stood guard against attackers and given their lives in order to protect their families. It is not difficult to recognize a wife's need for her husband's protection in dangerous situations, but often a wife misses the more subtle things that a modern-day husband might do out of his sense of protectiveness.

The following are some of the ways a husband today might express protectiveness toward his wife:

*   He makes sure the car is in safe working order.

*   He will try to buy or rent a home in a decent neighborhood.

*   He keeps the home in safe repair with strong locks on the doors.

*   He provides insurance and/or investment funds for his family's future.

*   He's there when his wife cries "help!"

*   He tries to shield his wife from evil influences that might harm her physically, emotionally, or spiritually. Protectiveness is why a husband sometimes objects when his wife watches certain TV programs, reads books he considers trash, or even when she spends time with certain friends. A husband may be aware that such "entertainment" will negatively influence his wife to fantasize rather than live in the real world, to become discouraged with her life, or to waste quality time.

*   He asks his wife not to get involved in, or at least to limit, certain activities (even worthwhile ones) because he knows her tendency to over-extend her energies. (This could include politics, community work, committees, and even church activities.)

* He chooses a church where the Word of God is faithfully taught and where he believes his family is protected from false teachers.

All of the above are expressions of a husband's protectiveness toward his wife and family. When he offers his hand as his wife steps off a curb, or when he opens a door for her, a husband is expressing the protective side of his manhood. If the small expressions of his protectiveness are rejected, he will begin to withdraw his protection entirely.

We are seeing more and more men today who have withdrawn their protectiveness toward women. I believe one reason is because several years ago many women began to reject even the simplest gestures of men's protectiveness. The women in this nation who were desperate to prove they didn't need men at all, started showing disdain when a man opened a door for them or took their arm when crossing a street. Later, these women began to force their way into many dangerous occupations that were traditionally dominated by protective men. Women now serve in such hazardous occupations as police and fire "persons," and in the military—soon they will be directly involved in front line combat. Women have been very instrumental in the desensitizing of men's feelings about the vulnerability of women. Today, many men (fortunately, not all) will just stand and watch as a woman struggles to lift and carry a heavy load. As men continue to lose their desire to protect woman-kind in the little ways, all women will become increasingly vulnerable to harm.

A wife can be an effective helpmate or an influence for her own destruction. If she discourages her husband from functioning as the leader, provider, and protector of his family, the effect is devastatingly destructive to his manhood and consequently to her own security. When a husband's manhood is damaged he can become a weak, effeminate man whose inability to protect his wife shames him in his own eyes, as well as in hers. Or, he can become an insensitive brute who is always trying to prove his superiority physically. On the other hand, a husband whose efforts are appreciated by his wife can develop a healthy masculine picture of himself as a "real man." The leadership, provision, and protectiveness of a "real man" enriches a woman's entire life and greatly increases her security.

CHAPTER XVIII

WOMEN AND WORK OUTSIDE THE HOME

Throughout human history most people have had to labor long hours every day just to be able to survive. Today, however, more and more of a family's physical needs are fulfilled by factories, department stores, grocery stores, and the services of other people. For instance, meat is butchered and cleanly packaged for us; staples come in boxes, bottles, and cans; and most produce is picked in the grocery store rather than picked from the garden. Prepared mixes and entire microwaved meals have retarded the American woman's tradition of talented cooking. The quality of home-grown and made-from-scratch has been traded for labor-free and speedy preparation.

Mass production has eased life for American men and women, but it has also altered the reason we work. Where we once worked producing the items we needed for survival, we now work for money in order to purchase those items. In addition, we work so that we will be able to acquire products and services that go far beyond our basic survival needs. Items that once were called luxuries—cars, larger homes, telephones, appliances, and clothing off-the-rack—are all products that modern Americans now consider absolute necessities. We also now pay others to do services that we once did for ourselves—child-care, housekeeping, and home maintenance, for example.

In this modern age the manual labor required for homemaking has greatly decreased, raising the question about whether wives really need to center their work exclusively around the home. Why shouldn't wives enter the work-place and gain more personal freedom and fulfillment, at the same time increasing the family's ability to buy more things? After all, a great deal of "work" today is more cerebral than physical. So, any woman who is able to acquire the required degree or training can conceivably fulfill most job requirements. Furthermore, work is no longer done for mere survival alone; it is now done for personal satisfaction and, of course, for the money. It is certainly true that the modern American family's perceived need for more and more money, in order to purchase more and more products, has long surpassed the earning capacity of most husbands. Many would argue that the two-income family is a modern necessity. But is this true?

It is difficult to give a definitive yes or no answer as to the biblical correctness of whether a woman should work outside her home. There are so many varied situations to consider— the woman who is unmarried, married without children, married with children, and a growing number of women who have children, but are not married. There may even be extenuating circumstances and variations within these groups. Rather than state a categorical position for all women I have chosen to provide a few guidelines to be considered, as well as discuss some of the distinct disadvantages that a woman must face when she chooses to work outside her home. This chapter is meant to provide you with enough information to evaluate the issue about working outside the home on an objective basis.

Considerations for an Unmarried Woman

Although a woman is intellectually and physically capable of handling many different types of work, there are numerous inherent disadvantages in certain occupational choices. A job that is not compatible with God's design for womanhood can jeopardize a woman's natural attributes and make her vulnerable to satanic deceptions. For instance, most of the women who support the feminist movement are career women who are highly educated in the world's vain philosophies, yet completely deceived about the advantages of biblical womanhood.

An example of an occupation that is not compatible with God's design is any field which would require a woman to compete against men for a controlling position. Any occupation that requires men and women to compete against each other creates a working atmosphere that is in reverse order to creation and puts an insufferable strain on the humanity of both sexes. Under such circumstances a man must overcome his natural protectiveness toward a woman and treat her as if she were just another man. My husband has spoken with several policemen who must constantly battle with their feelings of protectiveness in order to treat their female partners as if they were men.

Conversely, when a woman hardens her own natural femininity for the sake of her career, she is in danger of becoming headstrong, willful, and self-serving. She must curb her desire to please others and replace it instead with competitive aggression. Developing such characteristics may help a woman compete in today's workplace, but these traits also make it very difficult for her to remain truly feminine. A woman who becomes accustomed to competing with men has great difficulty turning off that aggressiveness at home. Such "reverse-order" careers can cause women to become the exact opposite of God's design for womanhood.

An unmarried Christian woman will want to consider the effect of her occupation on the success of a future marriage. It has long been known that men who work in high-adrenalin jobs (such as police officers) have a harder time living normal lives while off duty. In a similar way, women who have become accustomed to working in any highly stimulating job will find it difficult to later work happily at home. Just as the excitement level of video games causes little children to become bored with real life, a career full of deadlines and personal glory makes it difficult for a woman to "settle down" to the normal role of a helpmate. Years of personal glory and career activities can be as addictive as video games. Women who go into marriage and full-time helpmating directly from their parents' homes are much less likely to become "bored" than those who have become addicted to a career.

Before choosing any occupation, a biblical woman will want to seek God's purpose for the talents He has given to her. She will also want to be especially alert to any deceptive influence that Satan might use in order to lead her away from God's design for womanhood. As a general rule an unmarried Christian woman should choose an occupation that will exercise her gifts, but will not destroy her feminine characteristics. Occupations such as child-care worker, customer-service agent, nurses aide, dental assistant, church office assistant, and similar service-type occupations could actually help prepare a woman for her future role as wife and mother.

Considerations for a Married Woman Without Children

Most young brides are already working when they enter marriage and this is considered advantageous in today's economy. Many women believe that work experience may also be essential if a woman is widowed, or if her husband becomes disabled and unable to support the family. However, a Christian woman doesn't need to panic about preparing ahead of time for such a possible need. She can trust that God will prepare her sufficiently should the need arise. Many older women who have found themselves in need of employment have found jobs that required the very skills that they developed during thirty or more years of devotion to their husbands and children.

In spite of the monetary advantages, there are some distinct disadvantages when a married woman has an occupation outside the home. When a woman weds she elects a life-time career as her man's helpmate; therefore, if she works outside her home she has two careers—her job and her husband. This means that a married woman must juggle twice as many pressures on her time and energy as her unmarried sister. A wife with a career will constantly have an emotional struggle between her job and her role as her husband's helpmate.

Perhaps the greatest disadvantage for the working wife is that her occupation will usually cause her to develop a completely separate life from that of her husband. This separated life creates a conflict of interest with a wife's role as helpmate and will leave her with little time to develop as her husband's soul-mate. Such couples meet occasionally as they rush out the door to their separate events, but neither one of them play a very active role in the life of the other. As a result, their relationship becomes more like roommates rather than husband and wife. This is hardly a picture of the oneness that God desires in a biblical marriage. If a wife chooses to work outside her home, she must be doubly careful to avoid making her job more important than the development of oneness with her husband.

A biblical woman's first responsibility before God is to be a helpmate to her husband. Therefore, she will want any work that she does to be secondary to that first calling. Her husband's leadership, as well as his individual needs, is what should govern the type of work a wife does, if any.

The optimum situation for a biblical woman is that her work will aid and encourage (but not replace) her husband's responsibilities. Ideally, any work she does outside the home would be with her husband rather than in separate careers. The wives of farmers, men who own their own businesses, or missionaries and pastors find it natural to work with their husbands. It is not possible for every woman to work directly with her husband, but no matter what else she does it is vital that she remains under her husband's leadership. A biblical woman's work should not interfere with her role of helpmate.

Considerations for a Woman Who Has Children

It is my conviction that a biblical woman should make any sacrifice possible to be a full-time helpmate, mother, and keeper of the home. A recent survey of 1000 households in southern California encouraged me to believe that many working mothers share my conviction. The survey revealed that "80% of the mothers surveyed said they would quit their jobs, if they could, to raise their children at home." The survey also stated that "many respondents said they cannot live up to their ideals of even the most mundane family traditions, such as eating dinner together." Some social historians went on to say that the "findings reflect a 'new realism' about the financial and emotional toll that an 80-hour workweek inflicts on dual-earner families. We've reached a time when we're more realistic of what the costs are of full-time employment for two-earner families."[21]

This information is both the saddest and the happiest news I've heard in a long time. It is sad news because it means that the women who left home because they thought they were house-slaves have discovered that they are now work-slaves, and they recognize the freedom they left behind. It is happy news because it means that some of those women are recognizing the importance of motherhood and they are seeking ways to return home to their children. If enough women do return home then perhaps the next generation will look at the consequences of a dual-career family more rationally.

With that said, however, let me insert that I'm painfully aware that our country's epidemic divorce rate and our inflated economy require some mothers to work outside the home. Many mothers must work in order to survive and they have few, if any, luxuries. Some of them work because it is truly their husband's leadership decision, others because their husbands are ill or disabled, and many more because of divorce or widowhood.

There are several reasons that Christian mothers must work and I deeply sympathize with these women because of the stress that they must bear. The first thing a working mother must learn to cope with is that she cannot effectively cover two or three responsibilities at once. In order to work outside of the home the whole family must make many sacrifices. Much prayer and study of God's Word is needed in order for a working mother to be able to bear her additional burdens. Careful planning, time management, and God's gracious help will enable a working mother to still be a successful mother.

For those mothers who do have a choice, may I appeal to you to reconsider your priorities? There is no greater calling for a woman than the privilege of being a mother, but this privilege also carries grave responsibilities. A mother has elected to undertake a very demanding and time-consuming career. This career requires the same devotion and dedication as any other occupational choice. Sacrifice, long-term commitment, hard work, time, and a variety of skills are needed to be a successful mother. Children desperately need their mother's love, guidance, and protection, as well as her provision for their physical, emotional, and spiritual needs.

WARNING!

If you are a working wife and mother, do not use this book as your excuse to quit your job immediately. Do not make such a leadership decision by yourself! There are extenuating circumstances that must be rectified before it is possible for you to return home. And, the choice is not completely yours alone; it is also your husband's.

When a wife works outside the home the family becomes accustomed to what appears to be additional income, but usually debts are incurred simply because the wife's income allowed them. Once you and your husband are used to a life-style afforded by two salaries, it is very difficult to make a sudden change. Change is only possible if together you and your husband agree to reduce your debts and adjust your life-style in order to live within his salary alone. In most cases where there is a will, there is a way; but this way could take from six months to several years to fully accomplish.

The wife who wishes to stay home with her children should do some homework before she even approaches her husband with the idea of quitting her job. Careful planning, respectful presentation of that plan, and creative ingenuity on a wife's part may be all it takes for her husband's enthusiastic endorsement of her homecoming.

The first thing a working mother might do is sit down and figure out how much it costs for her to work. Let's face it, few women have careers that pay high salaries. Most women have jobs that barely cover the expenses incurred because of their work. I have seen several cases where both the husband and wife were shocked at how little money the wife actually took home. One such accounting that I've seen was a woman who was a real estate broker and earned $40,000 a year. Her accountant pointed out that she was paying 60% of her salary to federal income tax, social security tax, state tax, and other miscellaneous taxes. After she subtracted the cost of her extra clothing, child care, and other sundries required by work outside the home, she found that she actually cleared $8,000 per year. This revelation caused her to quit selling real estate and to engage in a home-style cottage industry. With her children's help she made arts and crafts and sold them at local swap meets. After expenses and taxes she netted $9,000 her first year.

There are many possibilities for mothers who need extra income. Some creative women have begun cottage industries in their homes. An added benefit has been that many of these enterprises have turned into family affairs. Other women have employers who have allowed them to take their work home. Some women have found that what they and their children gain through home schooling is worth the sacrifice of the little they earned, and certainly less expensive than day care and private schools.

Another Warning

If you have a strong conviction that you need to be home with your children, but your husband is unwilling, then it will be necessary for you to continue working. A situation such as this will be a difficult test of your character as you try to keep a correctly submissive attitude toward your husband's decision. Remember, God can use this situation to help you develop a deeper dependency on Him. It will help if you keep in mind that nagging, pouting, or otherwise punishing your husband for his decision is counter-productive to a biblical marriage. Pray that God will help you maintain correct biblical attitudes and that He will reveal to your husband both the need and the way for you to stay home with your children.

Some Questions to Ask Yourself

The following are a few basic questions that any woman may ask herself in order to determine whether her work is in keeping with God's design for womanhood.

* Does my work place me in greater danger of being influenced by false and deceiving philosophies?

* Is my work in keeping with the woman's design and God's stated will for women and their relationships with men?

* Must I sacrifice God's will to pursue this work?

* Why do I do what I do? Are my motives personal ambition, excitement, recognition, money, or is it because of God's will?

* Does my work create separation and friction between myself and my husband?

* Does my work cause me in any way to defy my husband's leadership and prevent me from being his helpmate?

* Does my work strengthen or weaken my husband's desire to be a biblical leader, protector, and provider?

* Does my work reflect responsiveness to my husband's leadership and does it fulfill his need for a helpmate? Have I sought my husband's leadership in the matter?

* Does my work interfere with my responsibility to aid my husband in teaching and training our children?

If you have to answer against the logical or biblical position to even one of these questions, your marriage relationship and your children are already suffering. If this is the case, I pray that God will reveal the way that you might remedy your situation. May you have God's peace of mind as you attempt to live according to biblical womanhood.

CHAPTER XIX

KEEPERS AT HOME

It has been said that the only absolutes in this life are death and taxes. However, after being a wife, mother, and keeper of the home for more than thirty years, I believe that there are at least three other absolutes. One, people cannot maintain healthy bodies for very long without proper nutrition, cleanliness, and protection from the elements. Two, just as soon as an object is cleaned it begins to get dirty again. And three, humans have emotional needs that are as important to their survival as any physical need. While meal times can be scheduled, human emotional needs must be filled by someone who is available at the exact moment the need arises. These three absolutes reveal the need for a dependable keeper of the home.

Although there has never been an invention that can substitute for the human touch in meeting emotional needs, we do have many excellent products that help people with the physical work of the first two absolutes. For instance, we have kitchen appliances to help us with nutrition, bathrooms and hot water heaters for sanitation, and houses and clothing to protect us from the elements. We also have products that simply make our lives more comfortable, such as furniture and carpets. However, no matter how many products we have that make staying healthy easier and our lives more comfortable, someone still has to shop for, store, and cook food. And someone must still clean the house, furniture, appliances, and clothing. For thousands of years the majority of these never-ending chores have been the responsibility of women. Why?

Some people believe that women have fallen heir to the cooking and cleaning because men didn't want the jobs. It is true a man simply can't do everything that needs to be done, so work must be shared. And, it also seems reasonable that a wife should cook the moose if her husband must go out and hunt for it. However, the real reason a woman is supposed to be the keeper of the home is because God appointed her to that position. A biblical wife is to be a helpmate to her husband, life-giver and teacher to her children, and she is to be a keeper of the home environment.

> *That they* (older women) *may teach the young women to be sober-minded, to love their husbands, to love their children, To be discreet, chaste, keepers at home, good, obedient to their own husbands, that the word of God be not blasphemed.*
> *Titus 2:4-5*

Until a few years ago, the standards for the American homemaker were in keeping with *Titus 2:4-5*. At that time homemaking was considered an absolute necessity for the health and welfare of the entire family. Women used their talents to make delicious and inexpensive meals from simple ingredients, and they turned even modest houses into warm and comfortable homes. Some women also understood that homemaking was much more than just cleaning a house and cooking meals. These women prepared their children for life, and they provided their husbands companionship and a respite from the world within their homes. Home was the center of a family's life. It was where all could gather for a hot meal and clean sheets, as well as for fellowship, understanding, and loving care. While it was a husband who usually built or purchased a house, it was his wife who gave that house a personality and transformed it into a home.

Today, many younger women have been convinced that their talents are too valuable to be kept at home. Instead, they believe that they should practice their talents in the marketplace and be paid cash for their efforts. The extra income that working wives earn may allow them to purchase a few more things for the house, but their modern houses are no longer warm and "alive" homes. Now, their houses stand empty most of the day and their latch-key children return from school to nothing more than cold electronics as a substitute parent. Today's children enter their houses to learn lessons of life from a television set, rather than from a real live and loving mom. They heat a snack in a microwave, rather than help Mom bake home-made cookies; and their fellowship is with their peers, rather than with parents who care. Many of our modern homes stand rich in prosperity, but very poor in soul.

There are no doubt many reasons for the drastic changes that have taken place in American homes over the last fifty years. Certainly one major reason has been the influence of humanistic philosophy, as previously discussed. However, two other important reasons are that women have lost their understanding of how important homemaking is to their families' welfare and that women do not have the self-discipline to work at home. For the past several generations young women have not been taught the art of making a home. Instead, they observed only the tedious work of house cleaning as their harassed working mothers delegated tasks in an attempt to do a week's worth of work on a Saturday morning. As a result, the word "homemaking" conjures up visions of repetitiously boring cooking and cleaning chores in the minds of modern young women. But, as we will see later in this chapter, there is much more involved in keeping a home than just cleaning the same nasty bathroom over and over again.

Younger women today equate homemaking with boring work, rather than with important work, so it isn't surprising that they have a mind-set against being a homemaker. Every woman wants to know that her labor is for a good cause. A woman who wishes to be a teacher will go to the trouble of obtaining a teacher's certificate, and she will work hard at being a good teacher because she believes that others will benefit from her efforts. Similarly, a young wife needs to understand that homemaking is valuable to her family's welfare and that she needs to dedicate herself to her role as keeper of the home. But, perhaps the biggest obstacle to homemaking for modern young women is that they lack self-discipline.

Self-discipline is a necessary attribute in every occupation. For instance, no matter how much a teacher may believe that her work is beneficial, there will always be some aspects of the job that she will not enjoy, such as the many hours she must spend grading papers. Because the teacher understands that her students will benefit from her labor she applies herself equally to the enjoyable activities of teaching, as well as to the distasteful tasks of paperwork.

No one is born with self-discipline, nor is it something that can be received from another. An individual learns the art of self-discipline by exercising self-control in order to overcome a weakness, such as laziness. The teacher who would much rather skip paperwork must use self-control in order to force herself to grade papers. Exercising self-control results in benefits for both the teacher and her students. First, the teacher becomes a more mature individual and a better teacher. Second, her students will benefit because grading papers helps her measure their progress and acquaints the teacher with areas where each student may need further training. Similarly, a woman and her family benefit when she exercises self-control and learns to do the work of homemaking. She gains personal maturity, and her family benefits because their physical needs are cared for properly.

A dedicated teacher does not equate teaching with only the drudgery of paperwork, and a wife should not equate homemaking with only the work of cleaning. Homemaking is a job, like any other job. It includes some work that is pleasant and other tasks that are not fun at all. A woman may love to cook, but hate to clean up the stove afterwards; nevertheless, she does the distasteful work because she knows it is important for the health and welfare of her family. Without proper nutrition and sanitation her family would be constantly ill. Therefore, a wife and mother will do the things that she enjoys **and** she will push herself in order to accomplish the less enjoyable tasks. Chores that are less than entertaining require self-discipline to accomplish, whether that work is done inside or outside of the home.

Warning

One of the problems with teaching any principle is that some people may misunderstand and take it to the extreme. At least three possible homemaking extremes that I'm aware of are the woman whose house is more important than the people who live in it; the woman who is a slave to others; and the woman who is extreme in trying to avoid both of the first two excesses. The woman who is excessive about housekeeping will try to keep "her" house looking as if no one lives in it. This woman will become very upset if someone walks on a carpet that she just vacuumed. The woman who is a slave to others believes that housekeeping is her job alone and she denies her children training in domestic chores. Such a woman encourages her husband and children to treat her as their personal maid. Meanwhile, the third woman goes to the opposite extreme. She thinks that anything and everything else has higher priority than a clean house. She rarely does housework and she even more rarely trains her children in household duties. All of these extremes are imbalances.

Being a balanced, biblical homemaker does not mean that a wife is the only one in the house who is able to vacuum a house or cook a meal. A wife may be the primary cook and bottle washer, but her husband and children should also know how to do the laundry, clean a bathroom and kitchen, and to care for themselves. (A husband **should** know how to take care of himself, but please remember another biblical principle—it is not a wife's place to try to pressure her husband about even that which he "should" do.) A mother should also remember that part of the biblical reason she is expected to be a keeper at home is so that she can train her children for their future lives. This includes teaching both boys and girls to take over their own physical maintenance and to be able to do house and yard work as young as possible.

Yes, But . . .

"Yes, homemaking is important to the welfare of a family, but . . .." What follows the "but" is usually something that seems to be a logical objection as to why a woman does not choose to be a homemaker. Most modern women believe that a wife has the right to choose between homemaking and working outside the home, regardless of God's Word, her family's needs, or any other factor. However, God's Word says that a wife **is** to be a "keeper at home;" therefore, a Christian woman who has chosen marriage and motherhood has already made her choice when it comes to the work of homemaking. Any work that a wife does outside her home is in addition to, and lesser in priority than her homemaking responsibilities. A wife cannot escape her biblical role as homemaker with, "Yes, but . . ." Nevertheless, it is necessary to discuss two objections against being a homemaker that are so common I've heard them over and over again. They are:

* "Yes, but I'm not the domestic type."

* "Yes, but I'm too talented, intelligent, and outgoing to 'just stay home' all day and be 'only' a wife and mother."

Let's analyze these two objections.

First Objection: "I'm Not the Domestic Type"

First, a woman **is** the domestic type simply by virtue of being born a woman. God designed women to be "nesters." Of the two sexes, women are normally the ones who intrinsically care about decorating their homes and they are the first to think of the physical needs of their families (proper nutrition, clothing, and health). Almost every bachelor's apartment I've ever seen desperately needed a "woman's touch," and their refrigerators contained little more than sandwich makings and moldy cheese. Most men appear to be perfectly satisfied with a comfortable chair, sheets on the windows, and a baloney sandwich—while women naturally care about how the furniture is arranged, pretty curtains, and a balanced diet.

Some women might say that they are not the domestic type as a plausible-sounding excuse for being inexperienced in the skills of homemaking. However, when a woman understands that being the keeper of the home is an important job, she can learn the skills. There is a list of recommended reading for learning the skills of homemaking at the end of this chapter. Knowledge, self-discipline, and on-the-job experience will also increase a woman's enjoyment of homemaking chores and ease homemaking phobia. However, let me add that making a home is not a cookie cutter kind of art where all homemakers must display the same proficiency in every area. For instance, one woman may love to sew all of her children's clothing, while providing her family very simple meals. For another woman the tiny details of sewing make her extremely nervous, so her sewing is limited to mending. But, she may spend a lot of time cooking because her husband loves fancy cuisine. Both women should know the basics of the art of sewing and cooking, but their individual talents, their husband's tastes, and their families' specific needs will direct each one to have a different homemaking style.

Second Objection: "Yes, But I'm Too Talented . . ."

"Yes, but I'm too talented (etc.) to just stay home and be only a wife and mother." The phrases "just stay home" and "only a wife and mother" reveal that some women think homemaking and being a mother have little value. Furthermore, it implies that only those women who are shy, have no talent, and possess very little intelligence could possibly choose to work at home. However, God never said for women to just stay home and vegetate. The homemaker in *Proverbs 31* looked after her home, but she never "just stayed home."

She looketh well to the ways of her household, and eateth not the bread of idleness.

Proverbs 31:27

Certainly, no one who has studied *Proverbs 31* could accuse this woman of a lack of talent or intelligence, nor could they say that she was "only a wife and mother." (See Chapter X.)

When a woman quits using objections that begin with "Yes, but . . ." and when she disciplines herself to do the work of homemaking, both she and her family will physically benefit. However, there is an added benefit that is perhaps even more important. A keeper at home is also close at hand when her family and friends are most in need of help.

I Timothy 5:3-10 reveals that a keeper of the home can involve herself freely in activities that offer physical, emotional, and spiritual help to others outside her home. Although this passage discusses the conditions under which the church may help a widow, it also provides us with information about what God values most in a homemaker. *I Timothy 5:4, 8,* and *16* state that a widowed homemaker is to be assisted first by her family, but that the church is to help if she does not have a family to care for her. However, the church helps only if the widow meets certain qualifications. A widow's trust in God, her personal character *(Verses 6, 7,* and *9)*, and works such as those below are part of her qualifications.

Let not a widow be taken into the number under sixty years old, having been the wife of one man, Well reported of for good works, if she hath

218

brought up children, if she hath lodged strangers,
if she hath washed the saints' feet, if she hath
relieved the afflicted, if she hath diligently
followed every good work.

I Timothy 5:9-10

There are other scriptural illustrations of homemakers helping others through their homemaking skills (not through meddling or self-righteous crusades). The women who housed and fed the disciples, traveling believers, the Apostles, and Christ Himself are examples of homemakers who were available to serve a ministry. After Jesus healed Peter's ailing mother-in-law, she rose and ministered to Him *(Matthew 8:14-15)*. Women such as *"Mary, the mother of John, whose surname was Mark" (Acts 12:12)*, opened their homes for early church meetings. Dorcus is an example of a woman who helped care for widows in their communities. Before Peter raised Dorcus from her death bed, *"the widows stood by him weeping, and showing the coats and garments which Dorcus made, while she was with them." Acts 9:39b*.

Balanced homemakers are valuable assets not only to their families but to their churches and communities as well. The *I Timothy* widow, as well as the *Proverbs 31* wife, worked to fulfill their roles as helpmates and mothers. Their families benefited, but so did strangers, believers, and the needy. These women were successful biblical women because they applied their minds and their talents to the role that God had designed for them.

A modern woman can be a successful keeper of the home, too. God gave every woman her own special talents and then He said for her to exercise those talents within her home. A woman is limited only by her own sin nature or a lack of willingness to apply herself to the task. Yes, a keeper of the home does have certain work responsibilities. She should cook meals that please her husband, do laundry, vacuum rugs, train her children, and maintain a peaceful home. More than anyone else she sets the atmosphere of the home and how she keeps it has an effect on all who enter her door. However, a homemaker is also privileged to teach her children moral and spiritual lessons, and she can patch feelings that have been hurt by the world better than anyone else. A keeper at home is her children's living example of biblical womanhood and her husband's ready companion. She is available when her neighbors are ill or when the widowed need her aid. A keeper at home is a woman whose "home-office" is located in a house, and her home is whatever she makes of it.

Recommended Reading

Is There Life After Housework? by Don Aslett. Published by Writer's Digest Books, an imprint of F&W Publications, Inc.. This book can be obtained through: Alpha Omega Publications, 404 West 21st Street, Tempe Az 85282.

Sidetracked Home Executives by Pam Young and Peggy Jones. Published by Warner Books, New York, NY, 1981.

The Creative Home Organizer by Emilie Barnes. Published by Harvest House Publishers, Eugene, Oregon, 1988.

CHAPTER XX

A WOMAN'S MINISTRY

Before the missionary began speaking he glanced at the fresh young faces that were eager to hear about the excitement of missionary life. He knew that the audience was made up of many who dreamed someday of being missionaries. He shocked his inexperienced audience and threw the cold water of reality on their romantic notions about missionary life when he began his speech, "If you aren't excited about going across the street to witness to your neighbor, what makes you think it will be any easier or more thrilling to go overseas?" This seasoned missionary knew the hard work, sorrows, and disappointments that are the realities of the mission field, so he wisely stated, "Like charity, missionary work begins at home. Those who are not willing to sacrifice should remain home." This is as great a truth for a woman as it is for a missionary—a woman's first ministry is at home. Those who are not willing to make the necessary sacrifices should remain unmarried.

Many wives and mothers today don't recognize the importance of their ministering at home. There was a time when I too viewed myself as "just" a wife and mother. I mistakenly believed that the mundane things I did at home contributed little to mankind and I wanted to do something "more" important with my life.

223

My mistake was that I believed highly visible crusades were all that God valued. I thought that only those who devoted their lives to the service of millions, like a Mother Theresa, were examples of being "in the ministry." Unfortunately, this misconception romanticized ministering away from home and discounted the value of the people closest to home. However, in time the Lord graciously lead me through the Scriptures to the knowledge that being a helpmate and a mother **is** a valuable ministry—and the one to which I had been called. It became very clear that my first ministry was with four very important people—my husband and my three children.

I intensely dislike using myself as an illustration. I have refrained in most cases because I am just another woman— not particularly intelligent or talented, and definitely a sinner. However, when it came time to write this particular chapter, it occurred to me that the "life resume" of an ordinary woman might help other women to see their own lives from a different perspective. For this reason only do I share a little of the ministry in my own life.

My Husband—My Ministry

Even though my husband is actually a very private and quiet person, God has made him a dynamic leader as well. In order to lead most effectively he has always needed a home where he can rest and escape from the stresses of his calling. While he is away from home, my husband also needs the assurance that the "home fires" continue to burn (without burning down the house). If he is denied this assurance he is unable to properly apply his mind and energies to his job. This means that I, as his helpmate, have a lot to do in order to assure him that all's well on the home front and to provide the type of restful atmosphere that he needs when he's home.

Thousands of people have been helped by my husband's leadership through his books, teaching, and management of Christian companies. The work that I do also helps those same people, just in a more indirect way. Like the head of a body my husband ministers directly; and like the muscles that keep the body strong, I minister indirectly. Though my work is mostly behind the scenes, my husband would not have the drive, time, or energy to do his work if I did not do mine. Therefore, by tending to the things that will help my husband I am freeing him to do his work.

My Children—My Ministry

Although they are now grown, my husband and I had shared a deep desire to help all three of our children develop into responsible adults. God entrusted three precious lives to us, and together we were responsible to *"Train up a child in the way he should go . . ." (Proverbs 22:6)*. God allowed me to see that training and ministering to my children was actually ministering to the whole of mankind as well. Turning three people loose on the world as untrained adults would have been a sin against God, as well as a gross injustice to my children and to our fellow man.

Words cannot express the pleasure that I now derive from the fact that my children are indeed responsible adults. However, I must add that the blessings I receive through my children are not due entirely to my own efforts. I am very human, with flaws and imperfections, and therefore I was an imperfect mother who committed many errors. Sometimes I was ignorant of what was right and sometimes I was weak, but God knew my heart's intent. I trusted that He would draw my children to Him—in spite of my failings—and He honored that trust. Today my adult children are law-abiding citizens and loving, caring individuals. They each have a personal relationship with Jesus Christ and they each care deeply for God's will to be done in their lives. Though they face the same trials and tribulations that all humans must face in this life, my adult children recognize the strong hand of God in every event, and they know from whom their deliverance will come. No outside ministry can provide a woman with more lasting joy than being able to witness her adult children willingly walk with the God who gave them life.

One Woman's Life Resume

In 34 years as helpmate, mother, and homemaker, I have held numerous positions and done a variety of work. The following are some activities that have been part of my ministry.

* Executive secretary and executive assistant to my husband's leadership responsibilities in three companies and one Christian school: Also, second in command of the "home office." Acted as overseer of three children and all home responsibilities. These responsibilities required: research on major purchases, budgeting, organization of schedules, progress evaluation, and reports to "upper management."

226

* Clerical work and bookkeeping: Simple accounting and record keeping for two businesses and a home. I'm the one who can locate last year's tax papers and the box that contains birth certificates and safety deposit keys.

* Money management: Purchasing agent, penny pincher, efficient shopper, and budget keeper. I have become an expert in stretching a dollar until it squeaks, and have found bargains that are virtually a steal.

* School Administrator: My husband and I ran a private school for two years. With the aid of self-instructional curriculum, I worked as a teacher for 23 children, grades 1-12. I was also the record keeper, purchasing agent of curriculum and supplies, as well as the designer of forms and procedures for school operations.

* Teacher: Taught my own children, a Sunday School class, many child evangelism classes, and other women about biblical marriage.

* Advisor: No psychologist can replace a wife and mother. I was a shoulder to cry on, a partner in laughter, an ear to strange and imaginative tales, and a prayer warrior with inside information. Encouraged, admonished, and exhorted my children; and, in addition, acted as a sounding-board, assistant, supporter, and best friend to my husband.

* Practical Nurse: Bandaged, taped, painted funny red medicine faces on hurt knees, and kissed minor physical injuries. Made soup, orange juice, read stories, sat up at night, rocked and otherwise nursed three children and a husband through a variety of illnesses.

* Food Manager: In this capacity I was dietitian, chef and fast-food cook, butcher, and baker; also planned, purchased, and prepared meals within a budget.

* Housekeeper: Laundry and cleaning. Yes, I did floors and windows as well as some other very messy and unappetizing jobs. I also headed and trained a staff of three assistants. These assistants became heads of their own departments as soon as they were able to manage their jobs.

* Interior painter and decorator: Painted walls and furniture, sewed curtains and bedspreads, and arranged furniture.

* Seamstress: Clothing, curtains, home decorating, doll and toy making, knitting, quilting, and other forms of needlework became my speciality.

* Hostess and Receptionist: Planned menus, prepared food, and served dinner parties, barbecues, and picnics. Acted as hostess for meetings and Bible studies, and opened our home as a hotel and diner for traveling friends.

* Volunteer: Worked part-time as a receptionist and record keeper for a husband and wife missionary team. Helped in a bookstore and volunteered in a hospital for a short period of time. Frequently filled in for vacationing secretaries and did other odd jobs in my husband's businesses.

* Pioneer: Lived for over one year in a mountain cabin heated by a Ben Franklin stove. Hunted for wild berries and other wild edibles; tried rose hips tea, jelly, and syrup, as well as dandelion greens and other interesting things. I baked bread and boiled tough squirrel while I learned to "rough it" without fast-food hamburgers. I was forced to became an expert at improvisation when I forgot to buy something on our weekly sixty-mile round trip into town. I also learned to cope with four feet of snow, three children and one dog who had puppies, as well as bears, raccoons, mountain lions, and other critters—in addition to five sets of down clothing, boots, mittens, a cabin that could never be cleaned, and our first year of home schooling. (I didn't live the life of a complete pioneer. Water from the creek behind the cabin was pumped into the cabin and all we had to do was keep the ice chopped away from the lines—and pray. We had electricity for lights and cooking as well as a telephone that didn't work during bad weather. We also had a four-wheel drive truck; however, I kept getting stuck in the snow anyway.)

* Today: I've written a book and this is the miracle of all miracles, accomplished only by the grace of God. His wonders never cease!

Not all women are alike. Each woman has her own unique talents and her husband has his own needs. However, whether a woman's husband is a business executive or a mechanic, he still needs the backing and support of his helpmate in order to be a successful employee, husband, father, church, and community member. And, a woman's children need their mother's love, care, and training. Beyond these two important ministries a woman who has the energy, time, talent, and permission of her husband, can also minister to others. The following are just a few suggestions where a woman might use her talents to minister to the needs of others outside of her home.

Administration

A woman who has a gift or talent for administration might organize a network of helps in her church (with the approval and leadership of her pastor) or neighborhood. She could organize groups of women who would be willing to minister to specific needs, such as a group of women to be prayer warriors, or a group who would provide transportation for the elderly or disabled. Then, when the need arises the organizer could call upon prearranged volunteers to fill that specific need. In this way prayer, meals, cleaning, transportation, visiting, babysitting, and much more could be provided quickly to the sick or needy. Another possibility for the woman who is talented in administration is to begin a cottage industry with her husband and/or children.

Teacher

A woman could home school her own children, and/or tutor other children from families who are unable to do it themselves. She could teach other women one of her own talents, such as painting or organizing time. Another possibility is training other women in homemaking skills like canning, sewing, baking, couponing, or money management.

Artist

An artistic woman could write, paint, sculpt, play music, or sing to the glory of God. She might also consider sharing her talent with others by teaching or through performances.

Helps

Many women are needed to assist administrators. A woman could provide physical help such as meals, babysitting, cleaning, and transportation to those in need. She could help her pastor and his family at stressful times or volunteer at hospitals, rest homes, or political campaigns. A church always has many needs a woman can fill: welcoming new people, making or distributing cassette tapes of the pastor's lessons to shut-ins, helping in the nursery, cleaning, or being prayer warriors, to name just a few.

Hospitality and Fellowship

A woman could organize other women for Bible studies, luncheons, and other fellowship gatherings. She could form a group who could exchange meals once a week or once a month. She might open her home to church or community functions, traveling missionaries, or other Christian speakers. She could also offer fellowship to the very shy, invalid, and other needy people who would be otherwise isolated.

Older Women

The older woman usually has talents and many years of practical experience that would serve well the members of her church. She is especially needed to teach younger women how to be sensible, pure, kind, and lovers of their children and husbands *(Titus 2: 4-5)*.

The opportunities for an older woman to minister to younger women are abundant. Most young women today are victims of a lack of parental training in self-control, contentment, frugality, homemaking skills, and parenting responsibilities—all of which are needed in the ministries of wife and mother. Frequently, these young women have come from homes where their mothers worked, or where their mothers felt trapped and resented their roles. As a result, the skills involved in making a warm home have become a lost art and the unselfish service of charity, wife, and mother a lost cause. This situation has created the false opinion among younger women in this country that being a homemaker means doing nothing and being bored. How we desperately need older women who will teach younger women the love and skills of homemaking. Unfortunately, too many of them are at the office.

The list you have just read contains just a few of the many possibilities where a woman might minister. It takes creativity, ingenuity, and imagination as well as dedication, self-discipline, and plain hard work to be a ministering helpmate, mother, homemaker, church, and community member. How a woman ministers depends entirely on whether she uses the mind and talents that God has given her, or whether she limits herself by closing her mind to the wide range of possibilities. A woman should always keep in mind, however, that God **never** leads her into a ministry that opposes her husband's leadership or denies his rightful needs. A grand and glorious ministry may get a woman applause and recognition from the world (or even from the church), but if it becomes more important than her husband, home, and children, it is not God's leading, nor does it bring Him glory. A woman who forsakes those within her home in favor of a ministry to others outside it, causes her home to lie empty, her husband to struggle without his helpmate, and her children to live as orphans.

You are a woman with at least one unique talent—praise God! By all means share your talent with your family and use it for the benefit of others. You are intelligent—praise God! Use your intelligence to think of all the possibilities that are available to you within your design. If you also are outgoing, again praise God, and use it to help others. But, before you begin any ministry turn first to the source of your talent and seek to use it in a way that is pleasing to Him. With prayer and Bible study, discover your talents and return them to God. Let Him lead you to where He can best use you for His glory and for His profit.

CHAPTER XXI

TO LOVE THEIR CHILDREN

Titus 2:4 instructs older women to teach young women *"to love their children."* This directive is particularly intriguing since most people believe that motherly love is intrinsic to a woman's nature. In fact, even most backward native tribes consider a woman abnormal if she does not display protective, motherly love for her children. Why then, does God say that a young woman must be taught to love her children? The only possible answer is that *Titus 2:4* is speaking of a different type of love than the kind that a woman naturally possesses. This chapter will explain the special type of love that must be learned, after first analyzing the characteristics of a mother's natural love.

Natural, Motherly Love

Motherly love is naturally responsive. Within hours of birth a mother and child are able to begin a rudimentary system of communication and response. This system starts with the baby's first cry, which brings Mom running. Crying is the vocabulary whereby a newborn communicates his or her needs, wishes, or state of being. For instance, a newborn has a hunger cry and a distress cry. By four to six weeks of age babies can control their vocal cords and they are cognizant enough to communicate frustration, as well as that fake cry that is actually a demand for attention.[22] A mother's natural responsiveness is the radar that enables her to interpret her baby's cries, noises, and gestures; and motherly love prompts her to respond to her baby's needs. There is no question that natural motherly love is necessary for the physical welfare of a baby. However, as important as this type of love is to an infant, it alone is not enough to train a child for adulthood.

Responsiveness in a mother is valuable, but it is also fallible. It is fallible because responsiveness alone is reactionary, non-thinking, and lacking in long-ranged discernment. Natural, motherly love responds on cue to what a mother emotionally "feels" is right and it prompts her to respond instantly with protective action. This natural protectiveness is important while an infant needs total care, but it can be extremely detrimental when a mother's sense of protectiveness prevents an older child from learning the harsher realities of life. A mother's instinctive love can cause her to have an unbalanced approach when it comes to child training. To obtain the results every mother truly desires for her child requires a love that exceeds natural, motherly care.

The Love That Must Be Learned

That they (older women) *may teach the young women to be sober-minded, to love their husbands, to love their children.*   *Titus 2:4*

The love that a woman must be taught is not a natural, emotional, or even protective kind of love. The love taught in

Titus 2:4 is based on the knowledge of what is right for a child from God's perspective. It is a love that requires thinking first and then acting in accordance with biblical truth for long-ranged results. A woman who loves according to a *Titus 2:4* love will govern her actions by what God says is right, rather than by what just seems right to her natural instincts.

The "older women" who understand biblical truths are supposed to teach "young women" how to love their children. The older women impart biblical information, as well as examples of their own successful results, so that the young women can develop a rapport with the truth about their children. Only by knowing and accepting biblical truths can any woman govern her natural affections and love according to a *Titus 2:4* love.

It is impossible in just one chapter to cover the entire subject of how a mother should biblically love her children. For a thorough understanding of this subject I must refer you to my husband's biblical expertise. Rick's book, *What The Bible Says About . . . Child Training**, is the most systematic development of biblical child training information available. It is essential reading for any mother who wants to learn how to biblically love her children. In this chapter I will only emphasize the importance of the father's involvement in child training.

---

* *What The Bible Says About . . . Child Training*, by J. Richard Fugate is available at most Christian bookstores or through Alpha Omega Publications, Inc., 404 West 21st Street, Tempe Az 85282.

Most mothers would agree that fathers are not involved enough with the training of their children. What can a wife do to encourage her husband to become more involved with child training? The answer is simple: be a biblically submissive wife, respect your husband's leadership, and don't interfere when he attempts to train the children. I cannot stress too much the harmful lessons that a mother teaches her children when she has a generally non-submissive and disrespectful attitude toward her husband, or when she openly challenges his child-training decisions or instructions. One of the biggest obstacles to proper child training, and the most damaging to children, is the disunity of the parents.

Conflicts with the Father's Training

One of the best ways to keep a father uninvolved is to interfere with his approach to child training. A mother's natural love and her desire to nurture her child can come into direct conflict with the father's objectives to train their child toward maturity. (It might be beneficial at this point to review Chapter VIII, "When Two Heads Are Better Than One.") Whenever a mother feels that the father is being unfair or too strict, her natural protectiveness will bristle. For instance, she may feel the father is unfair when he demands that their unwilling son mow the lawn on a hot day; or, she may feel that he is too strict when he requires their sobbing daughter to pay for a carelessly broken vase with money she had saved for a special dress.

A mother may feel that her son's comfort on a hot day or her daughter's emotions are more important than a mowed

238

lawn or an inconsequential vase. The father is probably not so concerned about having the lawn mowed on exactly that day, nor does he care if the vase ever gets replaced. What concerns him most is that his children learn valuable lessons for their rapidly-approaching adult lives. He wants the son to learn that work must be done even when it is uncomfortable, and he wants his daughter to learn that there are always consequences for careless actions. Sometimes a mother's protectiveness causes her to misunderstand the underlying reasons for her husband's child-training decisions. It can also interfere with valuable child training.

A mother's natural protectiveness will almost always cause her to feel that her husband's treatment of "her" children is at least occasionally unfair. However, whether or not her assessment is correct is not really the important issue. What is crucial is that the children learn to be respectful and obedient to their father's instructions, even when those instructions go against a mother's special sensitivity. Almost the cruelest thing a mother can do to her child is to openly challenge the father's instructions or punishments. (Of course, a mother should protect her child against true abuse, but she should not interfere when something her husband does just seems unfair to her.) **A child can get over an unfairness, but he will never get over lessons of disrespect that he learns from his mother.** I repeat, there may be nothing more harmful to a child's future than having his mother interfere with his father's training. Let's look at some of the things that a mother can teach her children just by the way she treats her husband's child-training decisions.

Do You Know What Your Children Are Learning?

Children are very observant and they learn a great deal just from what they see their parents do. For instance, they learn to respect or to disrespect their father by watching their mother's responses to him. If father says that the children are to do certain jobs around the house and mother makes sure they do them, the children learn that father must be obeyed, even when he is absent. A wife's cooperation (or lack thereof) will silently teach her children more lessons than her words can ever teach. Some of these lessons follow:

1. A wife can passively or actively interfere with her husband's instructions to their children. Passive interference might be in the form of forgetfulness. For instance, when she disagrees with her husband's instructions, she may "forget" to oversee the children's compliance. Her lack of submission will teach the children to "forget" whenever they wish to get out of complying with any authority. This tactic also can backfire on mother, because the children will forget to follow her instructions as well.

   Active interference is evident **anytime** a mother openly argues against, or defies, the father's instructions. The children will quickly follow mother's lead and they too will defy their father's authority. And, don't think that children cannot hear whispered disrespect, or read body language such as hateful facial expressions and resentful sighs—they can! When children even sense that their mother does not agree with their father they will very quickly learn to pit their parents against one another in order to escape the need for obedience.

On the other hand, a mother's cooperation with the father's directives will teach the children to respect and obey their father. As the children observe their mother's submissive attitude toward the father's authority, they learn to respect all other forms of authority as well. Respect for authority is one of the most important truths for mankind to learn! It affects one's relationship with God, with government and laws, with employers, and is central to God's plan for marriage.

2. A wife needs her husband's firmness in order to train their children, especially in the teen years. How effective her husband will be depends on whether she taught the children to respect and listen to their father's authority during their preteen years. When a mother challenges a father's right of authority, she completely destroys his future effectiveness with the children. However, when she teaches them to respect their father while they are young, the children will listen to what he says when they are older.

3. A daughter watches her mother's example of how to treat her future husband. By watching her mother's reaction to the father's decisions, she either learns how to be a supportive helpmate or she learns to be defiant and self-willed, just like her mother. Your

daughter's present attitude toward her father is a mirror-image of what she has observed and learned from you. It is also how she will likely treat her own husband in the future.

4.   A son also learns about authority by observing his mother. When a son is required to respect his father's authority, he learns to respect the position of authority in general. A son who understands authority will grow up to be a stronger leader himself. However, when the father allows his wife to show him disrespect and bows to her rebellion, his son will grow up to be weak like his father, or he will grow to hate his father for that weakness. A grown man who despised his father's weakness often fears that he too will be a weak man. In order to keep from appearing weak, that son may compensate by becoming over bearing on his own wife and family.

During his early, impressionable years a boy's mother is his only example of womanhood. Whatever he has seen in mom is what he later attributes to all women. A son who observes his mother's rebelliousness invariably winds up having an intense disrespect for all women in general. Perhaps this is because he inherently knows that rebellion is incorrect.

A mother who loves her children with a *Titus 2:4* love understands the necessity of stemming her natural, motherly responses in favor of her child's long-ranged good. Even when she feels that her husband is too strict, insensitive to her child's feelings, or unfair in his punishments, this mother knows that her child's respectful attitude towards his father is far more important than how he presently feels. Without early training and respect for the father, that seemingly sweet and sensitive child can become a self-willed, angry, hateful, and rebellious teenager—and his mother's bitterest sorrow.

> *The proverbs of Solomon. A wise son maketh a glad father, but a foolish son is the heaviness of his mother.* *Proverbs 10:1*

Only a mother who has suffered for raising a rebellious child can know the pain that mere words are insufficient to express. This is why I have dubbed the mother who insists on training her children according to her own natural emotions as the "play now-pay later" mom.

A biblical mother must learn to be a "pay now-play later" mom. The mother who learns to biblically love her children may pay some emotional costs while they learn to live rightly. But she will be securing her children's maturity, as well as her own peace of mind. The following is an example in my own life that may help encourage the reader to love her children with a *Titus 2:4* love.

My Own Struggle with Natural, Motherly Love

I can still feel the emotional struggle that I had when our son decided to leave home. At the time we were living in a house situated in a green valley surrounded by steep hills. It was a lovely home where meals were regular and where many other comforts were freely provided for all our children. Nevertheless, at age 17, with only his clothes, his bicycle, and a job at a fast-food restaurant, our son set off to make his own way in the world. On his salary, he could barely afford to pay for baloney sandwiches and rent, let alone buy such things as a car for transportation.

One particularly cold winter day, our son rode his bicycle into our valley to visit his worried Mom. When he was ready to leave, I watched him put on two sets of clothing and a knit hat over a ski mask before riding his bike to the apartment that he shared with two other young men. The wind was blowing icy sleet against him as I watched him bend low in an attempt to ride his bicycle up a hill that even cars were struggling to climb. My mother's heart bled because I wanted to protect him from such a hard struggle—but, I did nothing. Why?

The reason I did nothing was because months earlier, when he wanted to leave home, Rick decided that our son needed to learn early in life how to stand on his own two feet. My motherly protectiveness was fearful of our son's youthfulness and I pleaded with Rick (in private) to forbid our son to move out. However, my husband knew the lessons that this particular boy needed to learn in order to become a man, and he knew it was best to learn those lessons early in life. Although it hurt Rick as much as it hurt me, he had enough long-ranged love for our son to let him go.

I admit that at this time I thought my husband was wrong. My motherly feelings of protectiveness made it particularly difficult for me to refrain from wanting to baby my son in an attempt to make up for what appeared to me to be a wrong decision on my husband's part. Graciously, by this time in my life the Lord had taught me to trust Him with my loved ones and to trust His design for marriage. Therefore, as I watched my son ride into the icy wind that day, I again entrusted my son to God.

Several years (and many mother's prayers) later our son emerged as a truly fine man. God had used the trials that he faced in his early manhood to teach him a strong work ethic and to cause him to become a responsible adult who understands his own accountability.

Recently our son said that one of the most meaningful things in his childhood was that his parents put forth a united front that he could never skirt around. This adult son appreciated that he was never able to play on his mother's emotions in order to escape his father's lessons. As a child our son was required to obey his father with respect, and now as a grown man he respectfully allows the Lord to direct his life. I shudder to think of the type of man he might have become if I had interfered with Rick's decision those many years ago. I could have been instrumental in preventing our son from becoming the responsible adult he is today.

I could give many more examples of this same type of conflict between my responsive mothering instincts and Rick's fatherly objectiveness. There was the time that I sympathized with one of our daughter's fear of facing something new in her life, and her father forced her to confront that fear. There were the tears of both daughters that made me want to give in to their wishes, even though their father had already said "NO!" Instead, both of our daughters were taught to respect and obey their father, even if it was hard on both them and me. As a result, neither daughter dated anyone until the boy had first met with Rick's grilling, and neither daughter married until the men received Rick's permission. Most women would have a hard time believing how our daughters sat calmly and trustingly in their rooms waiting for their father's verdict. Both of our daughters were prepared for living biblical womanhood, because they first were required to respectfully submit to their father's authority.

How I thank God for supplying me with the biblical knowledge of how to love my children in a way that could surpass my natural instincts. The times that I may have been correct in my assessment of my husband's child-training tactics are inconsequential compared to the rightness of living in God's design. Only God's way can make everything come out right in the end. How much better off my children were when they were teens, and how much better off they are today, because of God's design for womanhood and marriage.

You too can love your children according to a *Titus 2:4* love. When a woman lives according to God's design for marriage she is offering her children the very best. God's omnipotence, omnipresence, and omniscience support His design, and His love is far greater than the mere natural love of any human mother.

CHAPTER XXII

VULNERABILITY TO SUFFERING

The woman said, "Let me get this straight. Biblical womanhood means that I voluntarily give up control of my life and place my entire future in the hands of my husband. No way! I'm not willing to be that vulnerable. My husband isn't completely mature, he's not always trustworthy, and he has far less common sense than I do. I can think for myself and don't need anyone else telling me what to do. I'm going to maintain control over my own life, thank you."

This imaginary woman senses that if a wife follows her husband's lead she may be led in a direction that might cause her to suffer. Her observations are positively correct. Men are capable of any conceivable sin or possible mistake. They can be inconsiderate and selfish or they can make mistakes, like getting involved in losing financial ventures.

Although this woman's insight is humanly correct, her decision to maintain control is spiritually very wrong. There are at least three errors in her reasoning that led her to an incorrect decision. First, she assumed that only she herself could protect herself against wrongful suffering. This woman's reasoning is flawed partly because no human being has enough power to protect themselves in this world. There are simply too many things that can happen over which a woman has no control at all. One only needs to observe the daily news to realize that we are constantly vulnerable to harm. Swirling around all of us are many unseen winds of danger that threaten our fragile human plans with tragedy. If a woman thinks she has the ability to protect herself from all suffering, she vastly overestimates her own power. Worse yet, she underestimates God's power to protect His own. Rejection of God's design never has and never will make a woman less susceptible to suffering. Help and protection from harm comes from the Lord to those who trust Him enough to live according to His ways.

> *Delight thyself also in the Lord, and he shall give thee the desires of thine heart. Commit thy way unto the Lord; trust also in him, and he shall bring it to pass.* *Psalms 37:4-5*

> *Cast not away, therefore, your confidence, which hath great recompense of reward. For ye have need of patience that, after ye have done the will of God, ye might receive the promise.* *Hebrews 10:35-36*

The second flaw in the woman's judgment is that she assumes she can reject God's design for womanhood and somehow escape any negative consequences for such an action. In reality, there is no better way to ensure suffering than to reject God's ways and to go one's own way.

*. . . Yea, they have chosen their own ways, and
their soul delighteth in their abominations. I also
will choose their delusions, and will bring their
fears upon them, because when I called, none did
answer; when I spoke, they did not hear; but they
did evil before mine eyes, and chose that in which
I delighted not.* Isaiah 66:3b-4

This passage reveals that the one who goes her own way
will actually bring to pass her own worst fears. For instance,
I know a woman whose husband was offered stock in his
company at a greatly discounted rate. However, this woman
was intimidated by her fear of loss and that fear motivated her
into preventing her husband from participating in his
company's offer. The result has been a loss of thousands of
dollars that would have secured their retirement today.
Hundreds of other examples of how a wife has interfered with
her husband's decision to begin a new business, or move in
order to obtain a better job, or to be more strict in the training
of their children could be given with the same type of
disastrous results. Vastly more Christians suffer from the
misery they create for themselves than those who suffer from
following God's plan.

The third flaw is the woman's assumption that suffering
unjustly is bad and must be avoided at all costs. Unfortunately,
this assumption is more common in the Christian community
than one might realize. Christians often fear that by doing
God's will they may suffer loss. Such fear causes many
people to ignore God's ways and to conform to the world out
of self-protection. For instance, fear of ridicule can cause a

Christian to cease witnessing, fear of ostracism can cause a teen to follow the crowd, fear of losing business can cause a man to be dishonest, and fear of her husband's mistakes or possible maltreatment can cause a woman to reject biblical womanhood.

A Christian woman should not allow fear to keep her from obeying God. Just as God can award the business contract to the man who will not be bribed, He can also bless the wife who follows her husband's immature leadership. However, if God does allow suffering in a biblical woman's life, we can be sure that He has also provided a way for her to be blessed through that suffering. Believe it or not, there are so many positive things that can come out of Christian suffering that believers ought to actually look forward to it, rather than try to avoid it. Let's look at some of God's positive reasons for allowing suffering to enter a Christian's life.

The Positive Side of Suffering

* It was necessary for Christ to suffer unjustly in order to provide us with a way of salvation.

   For Christ also hath once suffered for sins, the just for the unjust, that he might bring us to God, being put to death in the flesh but made alive by the Spirit.   *I Peter 3:18*

* Christ suffered to fulfill God's plan, and to bring glory to God. The unfair suffering in a Christian's life is for the same purpose.

252

But rejoice, inasmuch as ye are partakers of Christ's sufferings, that, when His glory shall be revealed, ye may be glad also with exceeding joy. If ye be reproached for the name of Christ, happy are ye; for the Spirit of glory and of God resteth upon you; on their part He is evil spoken of, but on your part He is glorified.

I Peter 4:13-14

* Christians should not be surprised when trials enter their lives.

Beloved, think it not strange concerning the fiery trial which is to test you, as though some strange thing happened unto you. I Peter 4:12

* Since Christians cannot expect to escape unfair suffering in this life, then suffering should be endured with the right frame of mind.

For this is thankworthy, if a man for conscience toward God endure grief, suffering wrongfully. For what glory is it if, when ye are buffeted for your faults, ye shall take it patiently? But if, when ye do well and suffer for it, ye take it patiently, this is acceptable with God.

I Peter 2:19-20

For it is better, if the will of God be so, that ye suffer for well-doing than for evil-doing.

I Peter 3:17

* Satan uses tribulation to tempt believers to fall, but God allows trials to strengthen believers and to cause them to stand.

Then Satan answered the Lord, and said, Doth Job fear God for nothing? Hast not thou made an hedge about him, and about his house, and about all that he hath on every side? Thou hast blessed the work of his hands, and his substance is increased in the land. But put forth thine hand now, and touch all that he hath, and he will curse thee to thy face.   *Job 1:9-11*

But the God of all grace, who hath called us unto his eternal glory by Christ Jesus, after ye have suffered awhile, make you perfect, establish, strengthen, settle you.   *I Peter 5:10*

* God has a good purpose for the suffering He allows in a Christian's life. He wants a Christian to go through suffering and become strengthened by it. He does not want a Christian to run from suffering and remain weak.

That the trial of your faith, being much more precious than of gold that perisheth, though it be tried with fire, might be found unto praise and honor and glory at the appearing of Jesus Christ.   *I Peter 1:7*

* Suffering is not something of which to be ashamed. Suffering can be the catalyst for spiritual maturity in the life of a believer, and it can be the means of spreading the love of God to others. This is equally true when believers suffer from problems in their marriages, as it is if they suffer from cancer.

And not only so, but we glory in tribulations also, knowing that tribulation worketh patience; And patience, experience; and experience, hope; And hope maketh not ashamed, because the love of God is shed abroad in our hearts by the Holy Spirit who is given unto us. Romans 5:3-5

* From God's perspective, trials are not disasters but rather opportunities to apply His power to real-life situations.

In famine He shall redeem thee from death, and in war from the power of the sword. Thou shalt be hidden from the scourge of the tongue; neither shalt thou be afraid of destruction when it cometh. Job 5:20-21

There hath no temptation taken you but such as is common to man; but God is faithful, who will not permit you to be tempted above that ye are able, but will, with the temptation, also make the way to escape, that ye may be able to bear it. I Corinthians 10:13

* Suffering teaches believers that worldly things are far less important than their relationship with Christ.

Not that I speak in respect of want; for I have learned, in whatever state I am, in this to be content. I know both how to be abased, and I know how to abound everywhere and in all things I am instructed both to be full and to be hungry, both to abound and to suffer need. I can do all things through Christ, who strengtheneth me.
Philippians 4:11-13

* Tribulations on earth are temporary and insignificant compared to the eternal values that they produce in the believer.

For I reckon that the sufferings of this present time are not worthy to be compared with the glory which shall be revealed in us.
Romans 8:18

For our light affliction, which is but for a moment, worketh for us a far more exceeding and eternal weight of glory.
II Corinthians 4:17

The verses above are only a portion of the **many** scriptures that teach a Christian about the positive side of suffering. I highly recommend reading Joni Eareckson Tada's book *Joni* for a more in-depth study of suffering. Suffering is something Joni knows quite intimately. She has endured trials that make

256

most of our problems appear insignificant by comparison. The principles in her book apply equally as well to minor marriage difficulties as they do to major tragedies.

In Conclusion

Yes, a woman places herself in a vulnerable position when she voluntarily submits herself to her husband's leadership. She becomes vulnerable not to a man but, to God's plan for her life. She also places herself in the best possible position to glorify God, as she utilizes His power during any suffering that she might experience because of following that plan.

The woman who lives according to biblical truth may appear weak to some other women but, actually she could never be stronger. The vulnerable woman can experience God's power in ways that those who renounce His design will never know or understand. If biblical womanhood opens us up to ridicule and rejection from the world, and if it makes us appear weak and vulnerable, then so be it! All the better for His power to shine through to those who seek God.

> *And He said unto me, My grace is sufficient for thee; for my strength is made perfect in weakness. Most gladly, therefore, will I rather glory in my infirmities, that the power of Christ may rest upon me. Therefore, I take pleasure in infirmities, in reproaches, in necessities, in persecutions, in distresses for Christ's sake; for when I am weak, then I am strong.*
>
> II Corinthians 12:9-10

CHAPTER XXIII

FROM THE PAIN OF TRIBULATION
TO THE JOY OF THANKSGIVING

The telephone rang on a particularly beautiful Arizona morning while Rick and I were sitting on our patio simply enjoying each other's company. The caller was a young woman who had separated herself from her husband a few months earlier. With a kind of weariness in her voice she asked "What are you doing?" I replied, "Rick and I were just enjoying our morning coffee outside on the patio." Sadly, she said, "Oh, how nice. I wish my husband and I could have had companionship like that."

At that moment my mind flashed back over the thirty-some years that Rick and I have been married. I envisioned those years as a trip that began on the day we wed and will continue until one of us goes to meet the Lord. Rick and I have traveled a very long and sometimes turbulent path together. There were plenty of sunny years, but there were also dark and cloudy years where the dream of peaceful mornings on a patio would have seemed an impossibility. How I wanted to tell my young caller that Arizona mornings don't just happen. The path to such peaceful times is like a toll road, and the fare is persistent endurance through many years of both pain and pleasure. If a woman is not willing to pay the toll, she cannot acquire the type of long-term companionship that Rick and I have developed through our years of common knowledge and experience.

How did Rick and I get to our Arizona patio? The funny thing is that we didn't ever want to live in Arizona. Although we were positive that the Lord wanted us to move there, our feelings about the move were similar to the Israelites when they said to Moses, *". . . because there were no graves in Egypt, hast thou taken us away to die in the wilderness?" Exodus 14:11b.* Needless to say we sold our belongings, packed our bags, and moved to Arizona with very heavy hearts.

Before coming to Arizona, Rick and I thought the desert was nothing but dry parched air, scorpions, unbearable heat, no water, land that could grow little but cactus, and unknown suffering. However, we have discovered that the dry air is good for us, the heat actually feels good (most of the time), and ten months of the year it is almost like utopia. As for the cactus and no water, God supplied us with a home where we have orange, grapefruit, lemon, and fig trees; and the back yard sets on a lake. We even discovered that the desert is a beautiful place where the cactus blooms in the spring and where dust particles in the upper atmosphere produce the most beautiful sunsets that we've ever seen. We have grown to love our home in Arizona more than any home we have ever had. What God has provided for us is proof that even when things look like our worst nightmare, the outcome can still be peace and blessing.

Arizona mornings are standard for Rick and me today, but it was not always like that. We were married when I was seventeen and Rick was eighteen. Not only were we young and immature, but we were unbelievers who were rebelling against our parents—not exactly the most solid ground on which to begin a marriage. You can probably imagine the troubles that we got ourselves into during the beginning years of our marriage. However, those troubles turned out to be for our benefit because they brought us to our knees and prepared us for the realization that we needed Christ.

Rick and I accepted Christ after ten years of marriage, three children, and many mistakes. Virtually from the beginning of our new birth, God started us on a crash course of learning His Word. While He was beginning to strip us of our alien, human thinking and replacing it with His own, we tried to stay at least one step ahead of our children in order to train them in the Lord. It wasn't always easy, but it was probably the happiest time of my life. I was excited about the Word of God and there was so much purpose in our lives. Little did I know that God was using those sunshine years of learning His Word as a prelude to a test that would shake my very foundation.

My Personal Testing

In my sunshine years I did not fully realize that learning **about** the Bible and **living** it are two different things. During those years of Christian childhood, I could talk excitedly about the doctrine of absolute dependency on the Lord, but my talk was as idle chatter because in reality I was depending more on Rick than I was on God. For my own good this unhealthy allegiance to a human being had to be reversed, and my dependency on God alone had to become total and complete. To this end, God allowed certain events to occur where Rick was removed as my life-line, and God was "all" that I had left.

The exact details of the events that shook my foundation are of little importance, except to say that they caused shock, fear, humiliation, and extreme suffering for both my husband and myself. For a while Rick failed me, I failed him, and we both failed our God. There were times when the only thing we did right was to hang in there, stay together, and keep returning to the Lord.

There really aren't words for the pain that I felt during those terrible years. It was similar to having major surgery without an anesthesia. There were times when I was in such turmoil that my chest hurt and I thought the lump in my throat would actually choke me. I can't recount all the times that I felt rage and anger. Frequent were the times I cried until there were no tears left and I heaved dry sobs. Once in a while I was so desperate that I even begged God to take me home.

Does that shock you? Please don't let it. This book has not been written by someone who thinks that she has always lived life perfectly, but by a human being who relates to failure and the pain of suffering that is common to all of us. In fact, this book could only have been written after God took my crushed pride, shame, fear, weakness, and total failure and used them to teach me His forgiveness, as well as the dependability of His character and His Word. Without those lessons, anything I might have written would have been just another academic study and I would never have had the confidence to say, "Yes, biblical womanhood **can** be lived in this modern world!" This book is my unwavering testimony that God can transcend any human experience and that He is there for His suffering children when they turn to Him. It is my grateful song of joy for what God did and what He taught me through the pain of personal tribulation. Before my struggle with pain and suffering, I only **said** that God's ways work, but after experiencing Him repeatedly honor His Word I **know** that they work.

God first taught me His Word and then He gave me ample opportunity to apply His ways to real life. Through personal tribulation, failure, as well as some successes, He allowed me to learn many valuable lessons. In addition, I have learned a great deal from others who have suffered. The following are some of the lessons that I have gleaned through my years of study, experience, and observation. I have learned there are some very definite do's and don'ts during suffering situations, and I have seen God work through human pain. If my eye-witness accounting can help other women as they go through life's trials, then I have one more reason for thanksgiving to God.

Thoughts of an Eye-Witness to God Working Through Pain

* Don't run away! There were many times that I felt like giving up and running away. However, God does not want us to run from our problems, He wants us to let Him carry us through our troubles. Going through

marriage troubles is a test of fire that is very painful, but when the pain is endured the final result can be a marriage that is better than what it was before. Emotional love is kid's stuff compared to the love that passes through the test of fire and emerges sharper, cleaner, and stronger.

* One of the most effective ways to have one's own character purified is during intense suffering. Trials and tribulations have a way of revealing who we really are, both bad and good. During troubled times, such flaws as pride can stick out like a sore thumb and unknown strengths, like the ability to forgive and forget, can emerge.

* God's plan is so complex that He can use a singular trial and tailor it to meet the needs of every person involved. It is God's desire that every believer grows to be more Christ-like. However, each individual has her own set of flaws that must be chipped away, as well as her own strengths that must be refined before she is a finished work. For one person the adversity may be chastisement for a sin, while for another the same adversity may be an opportunity to practice longsuffering and Christ-like forgiveness.

* Trials often help to develop a true biblical love. True love loves the unlovely, gives to the selfish, remains faithful to the unfaithful, and forgives the unforgivable—just like God's love.

Prayer Is Essential, Not Optional

* I saw God work in my life more during my suffering than at any other time in my life. My prayers were more regular and intense. I found that my mind was more alert to God's presence and my heart was more open to His love in my pain.

There are many advantages to prayer. When a woman is in open communication with God she is in the optimum position to see Him work beyond all human limitations. It isn't that she will escape all fear and pain, but that she will learn to let God carry that fear and ease that pain.

* Prayer has a calming effect on the soul and brings frustrations into perspective. Prayer slows down a woman's emotional reactions to problems and it increases her ability to mentally focus on solutions that are more Christ-like.

* Serious trials cannot be overcome in the power of the flesh. They must be endured God's way and with His power. Consistent prayer, acknowledgement of sin, and commitment to being a "doer of the Word" is a daily must.

* Don't be afraid to tell God exactly how you truly feel. It seems some people think that all God ever wants to hear are pious prayers. However, if you bury or deny that such things as anger or bitterness exists how can

these negative feelings be dealt with? Certainly, the
writer of *Psalm 77* understood how to pour his true
feelings out to God in prayer.

> *I cried unto God with my voice, even unto God
> with my voice, and He gave ear unto me. In the
> day of my trouble I sought the Lord. My sore ran
> in the night and ceased not; my soul refused to be
> comforted. I remembered God, and I was troubled;
> I complained, and my spirit was overwhelmed.*
> *Psalm 77:1-3*

* Disclose every evil thought you have to God; He knows
  them anyway. Today, I can almost laugh at the times
  I virtually ranted and raved to God. I learned to tell Him
  how angry I was or how much I really didn't want to
  do the right thing anymore. However, no matter how
  loudly I fussed, when I was through haranguing, God
  turned my mind to His absolute power and goodness.

> *Thy way, O God, is in the sanctuary; who is as
> great a God as our God?*   *Psalm 77:13*

After such "discussions" with God, He always gave
me the strength to keep on keeping on for one
more day.

* Pray without ceasing. Pray for an end to your suffering,
  but do so with a willingness to accept God's will and
  His timing. Too often we make up our minds ahead of
  time that what we want is what God wants. This is

266

not necessarily so. For instance, a woman may be suffering because she wants a child, and her husband does not. Because she assumes that God wants what she wants, she **tells** God to make her husband want a child. This woman is not praying for God's will; she is dictating her own will. When you go to God in prayer, do so with a desire to discover, and a willingness to accept, His perfect will.

WARNING: Things to Avoid During Marriage Conflicts

* Ann Landers often tells a troubled wife to ask herself this question: "Would I be happier without my husband than I am with him?" This type of advice is humanistic, me-centered, and promotes the philosophy that one must live only for the happiness of today. While a person is in the depths of an unhappy situation, she will almost always think that the grass looks greener on the other side of the fence. However, the grass really isn't greener and if you run away from your problems, you will probably end up repeating them or creating worse problems. If you start thinking that divorce is an option, it will probably come to pass. Dr. Diane Medved's book *The Case Against Divorce*, as well as other recent findings, reveal that most divorced men and women later confess that "knowing what I know now, I probably could have made it (their marriages) work."

During marriage problems it is important to avoid thinking that the pain of today will last forever. Instead, with prayer and thanksgiving, trust that God can make the impossible happen in due time.

*   Don't worry if you feel that you don't love your husband at the present time. When a woman is tired, discouraged, angry, or hurt, her thoughts tend to be very self-centered. In this state it is impossible to love anyone else. It's hard to emotionally love the person who is causing you to hurt. Don't insist that your marriage is over if you, or even your husband, do not presently "feel" in love. Get things right between the two of you and in due time you will love again.

*   Be careful of your husband's reputation while talking to friends. Your husband has a right to his privacy. Don't go into great detail about what a failure your husband is or dramatize his words and actions. Consider the effect on your husband's reputation if your friend tells others (and they usually do tell at least one other). Gossip has a way of sticking around for years. It leaves its dark impression on the minds of those who hear it and that impression is often never removed. Even years after you and your husband have made up and you have completely forgotten what you said, others will still remember.

*   Be very careful with whom you talk about your problems. There is nothing wrong with seeking help, but don't talk indiscriminately to just anyone. Many divorces have been encouraged by "helpful" and "loving" friends who cluck their tongues and foster a

268

wife's feelings that she is a suffering saint. Be especially wary of "support" groups where other unhappy women make you feel good about yourself while they promote your stepping outside God's design for womanhood. These groups usually encourage a woman to arrogantly defy her husband's leadership, or they urge her to separate and finally to divorce her husband. If your advisers do not help you understand how God's design for womanhood applies to your particular problem, then beware of following their advice.

Any advisor that you consult should have certain qualifications. First, the counselor should be a mature, biblical Christian. Second, you need someone who will support you as you apply God's Word to your particular situation, not someone who will just agree with what a jerk your husband might be. Your best choice of counselors would be a husband and wife team or an older woman from your church.

*   Be extra careful about being alone with another man (pastor, counselor, or friend). You are especially vulnerable to the attentions of a man when you are suffering. Furthermore, men are exceedingly vulnerable to a damsel in distress. If you cry on a man's shoulder he may begin to feel protective toward you and you may respond to his attention with such appreciation that either of you could misinterpret your feelings to be love. You could be starting something that should never be!

* A woman's mind is similar to a video recorder that tapes memories. When a woman suffers she tends to replay those recorded memories inwardly and she relives every hurtful thing her husband has ever said or done. Playing with these mental images is a little like playing the old game of gossip. Each time the gossip is repeated the story is dramatized and embellished until it no longer resembles what actually took place. Such mental games actually create new pain as a woman's mind takes past events and projects them into the present. As memories of yesterday's pain are piled on top of new disappointments, the original events or words become distorted and the intensity of the present offense is multiplied. Women who have played these negative memory games for years wind up bitter, angry, and more than a little self-righteous.

Each time you remember something that emotionally hurts, refuse to play with it in your mind and turn to God in prayer instead. You might also read your Bible, replay good memories of your husband, exercise, go bowling, play tennis, talk to a cheerful friend, or almost anything that will divert your attention from negative thoughts.

* Avoid listening to country and western music or doing anything that will make you more depressed and feeling more sorry for yourself.

* Don't watch soap operas, love-triangle stories, daytime talk shows, or other programs that promote the idea that all men are evil and selfish creatures. Your emotions are already tender and these shows can only cause you to relate to other women's problems as if they were your own. One hour of this kind of bonding with "other mistreated" women and you can be primed with self-righteous indignation and ready for battle the minute your husband walks through the door.

* Be very careful about what you read. Reading romance novels promotes the development of fantasies about men and marriage. No real man can live up to a romance novel's description of a sensitive and debonair Prince who sweeps a damsel off her feet.

In Conclusion

When a woman is suffering marriage problems, it is very difficult for her to accept that the best way to solve those problems is to continue to endure suffering. No one wants to hear such advice. It goes against the sin nature's tendency to either fight for one's rights or to flee from pain. Although I understand the human desire to escape pain as quickly as possible, I also know that neither fight nor flight is God's way to deal with the suffering that He allows in our lives. Instead, He desires for His children to be delivered from adversity by, and through, His might.

Ye shall not need to fight in this battle; set yourselves, stand ye still, and see the salvation of the Lord with you . . .   *II Chronicles 20:17a*

God wants Christians to bear up under difficulties by exercising longsuffering love and by holding on to an unshakeable trust in Him.

> *Love suffereth long, and is kind; love envieth not; love vaunteth not itself, is not puffed up, Doth not behave itself unseemly, seeketh not its own, is not easily provoked, thinketh no evil, Rejoiceth not in iniquity, but rejoiceth in the truth; Beareth all things, believeth all things, hopeth all things, endureth all things.*
>
> *I Corinthians 13:4-7*

He wants to carry us through our suffering and bring us to a place where He can pour out His blessings. Only in this place does the pain begin to make sense and is suffering finally traded for the joy of thanksgiving.

> *But thanks be to God, who giveth us the victory through our Lord Jesus Christ.*
>
> *I Corinthians 15:57*

One time long ago, when I was under such intense pressure that I could not concentrate long enough to pray, I would write out my prayers. Writing letters to God seemed to help me express my thoughts better. For some reason I kept one of those prayers. Perhaps it will help other women who are presently suffering if I share it now.

> Heavenly Father, you know my heart is troubled. You know my weakness and my sorrows.

272

Father, remind me of your wisdom when I am in my own human thoughts.

Remind me of your sovereignty when I feel a loss of control.

Remind me of your grace and mercy when I am angry with others.

Remind me of your presence and loving care when I feel alone.

Grant me peace and calm during my troubles and help me to remember I am cradled in your everlasting love.

Give me your strength in order to withstand all that is happening and strength to endure the future.

Oh, how I thank you Father for your forgiveness for my sins. I know your hand is stretched out to all who turn to you and I thank you. I thank you ahead of time for answering this prayer.

In my soul I hold fast to your hand for guidance and for a steady foot as I walk through my valley of pain and tears.

Even though I often falter Father, I pray that you will still be glorified and that ultimately your will will be done in my life.

I thank you for the peace of knowing that you have all things in control and that you will always do what is best for everyone concerned. In Jesus name, Amen.

This prayer was answered in every way!

Thou has turned for me my mourning into dancing; thou hast put off my sackcloth, and girded me with gladness, To the end that my glory may sing praise to thee, and not be silent, O Lord, my God, I will give thanks unto thee forever.

Psalm 30:11-12

CHAPTER XXIV

HELP! I'VE DONE EVERYTHING WRONG!

This chapter is for the woman who feels that she has already failed so completely that recovery is hopeless. She may be divorced and now feels crushed by the realization that she could have made her marriage work if she had only understood biblical womanhood years earlier. Or, she may now recognize that her present marriage problems are due largely to her own violation of God's design for womanhood. No matter what the reasons for her feelings of failure, she can take hope that hers is not a lost cause.

With God there are no lost causes. If there were truly a hopelessly lost cause, I imagine Paul would have been such a one. Before his conversion, Paul consented to the stoning of Stephen *(Acts 7:58-8:1)* and he enthusiastically persecuted the early church. What Paul did to the early Christians was probably the reason that Paul called himself **"chief"** among sinners in *I Timothy 1:15*. Paul might have carried a tremendous sense of hopelessness and guilt forever, except that he understood the abundant grace of God.

> *. . . But where sin abounded, grace did much more abound; That as sin hath reigned unto death, even so might grace reign through righteousness unto*

eternal life by Jesus Christ, our Lord.

Romans 5:20b-21

Paul has not been the only one who has been elevated to the heights of victory by God's grace. *Hebrews 11* provides a comforting historical record of some other sinful humans whom God raised above failure. Those people failed in diverse ways (everything from murder to prostitution) but they each succeeded in only one way. Everyone of them conquered their particularly impossible situations by placing their total trust in God. They then attempted to live day by day in obedience to God.

As it was for the people in *Hebrews 11,* so it is for a Christian woman today. A woman's future success is not dependent on her past failures, nor is God's plan for her life terminated by any presently difficult situation. A woman's future is dependent solely on whether she will entrust herself to the abundant grace of God today, and everyday from this point on. The following are three essential steps in correctly entrusting oneself to the grace of God.

Entrusting Ourselves to the Grace of God

Step One: A Prayer of Confession

> *If we confess our sins, he is faithful and just to forgive us our sins, and to cleanse us from all unrighteousness.*   *I John 1:9*

Confession of any known sin is always the first step when we become aware that we have sinned against God. This includes adultery, divorce, lack of submission, or any other sin. Confession cleanses us of sin and prepares our minds for the second step.

Step Two: Forgiveness of One's Self

> *. . . but this one thing I do, forgetting those things which are behind, and reaching forth unto those things which are before, I press toward the mark for the prize of the high calling of God in Christ Jesus.*   *Philippians 3:13a-14*

Accepting the total forgiveness of God by also totally forgiving herself for any past sin is essential before a woman can completely entrust her future to the grace of God. She cannot confidently progress if her mind is weighted down with guilt over the sins of the past.

Step Three: A Total Commitment to God's Ways

> *Knowing this, that our old man is crucified with him, that the body of sin might be destroyed, that henceforth we should not serve sin.*
>   *Romans 6:6*

> *I beseech you therefore, brethren, by the mercies of God, that ye present your bodies a living sacrifice, holy, acceptable unto God, which is your reasonable service. And be not conformed to this*

world, but be ye transformed by the renewing of
your mind, that ye may prove what is that good,
and acceptable, and perfect, will of God.

Romans 12:1-2

This third step is sometimes omitted when people speak of the grace of God. Some believers wrongly assume that since grace abounds and covers all past sins that a Christian woman can just continue to disobey God's design for woman hood and marriage. Not so!

What shall we say then? Shall we continue in sin,
that grace may abound? God forbid. How shall
we, that are dead to sin, live any longer in it?

Romans 6:1-2

God forbid that a Christian woman should knowingly continue in any disobedience of God! Arrogantly taking advantage of God's grace is not the same as entrusting oneself to the grace of God. God's grace wipes out a woman's past failures and even delivers from her present deficiencies, but it is not a license to sin.

And God is able to make all grace abound toward
you, that ye, always having all sufficiency in all
things, may abound to every good work.

II Corinthians 9:8

A Closing Message for You

Can **you** live biblical womanhood in today's world? Yes, you can! You can because your ability to live biblical womanhood does not depend on your past or your present circumstances. It does not depend on your perfection; but instead, living biblical womanhood depends entirely on God's perfection. God designed a specific purpose for a woman, He has commanded a believing woman to live according to that purpose, and He bestows the power to accomplish His purpose in her life.

Today can be the first day of your new life! You can move forward from this point on and know that God loves you, that He has forgiven you for all your past sins, and that you can trust Him to be with you today as you obey His design for womanhood. If you are presently having marriage problems, simply begin today to live according to the principles of biblical womanhood and trust that God will show you how to mend your marriage. If you are separated or divorced from your husband, and neither of you have remarried, pray that God will make it possible for the two of you to be reconciled. Approach your husband with what you have learned and ask for his forgiveness for the part that you played in your separation.

If you are divorced and have no possibility for reconciliation because of remarriage, then forgive yourself for the past and trust God for your future. If you are remarried, then begin today to make your present marriage a biblical one. Whatever your present circumstances, no matter how black or how bright your future appears to you, commit your life to the grace of God. Begin living biblical womanhood today and trust God to bring about His will in your life.

> *So shall my word be that goeth forth out of my mouth; it shall not return unto me void, but it shall accomplish that which I please, and it shall prosper in the thing whereto I sent it.*
>
> *Isaiah 55:11*

Some women may still be hesitant to take the first step of committing themselves to living biblical womanhood. If this is true for you, you will need to prayerfully reread this entire book with a highlighter in one hand and your Bible in the other. In fact, no matter what your circumstances are today, you may need to read this book at least once every year or so as you and your marriage mature. In between, keep the book handy for those specialized times when you need to refresh your memory. With each review, you will gain a deeper understanding of how to apply biblical womanhood to your own life. On the following page is a topical list to aid you in reviewing specific subjects.

Review List

1. For a better understanding of your husband's drives to lead, protect, and provide for his family, review: Chapters II through IV, VII, VIII, and XIV through XVII.

2. For a better understanding of why you need your husband's authority and leadership, review: Chapters III, IV, and V.

3. For a better understanding of God's design for womanhood, review: Chapters II through IV, VI, VIII through X, and XVI through XXI.

4. For a better understanding of the difference between submission and obedience, review: Chapter VI.

5. For a better understanding of the powerful influence you have on your husband, review: Chapters VII through IX.

6. For a better understanding of how to communicate with your husband, review: Chapters XIV and XV.

7. For recognizing and defusing the influence of Satan in your life, review: Chapters XII and XIII.

8. For understanding why pain and tribulation cannot be completely avoided in your life, review: Chapters XXII and XXIII.

9. For understanding how to deal with your husband if he doesn't appear to be cooperating with your efforts to build a biblical marriage, review: Chapters XIV through XVI.

10. For patience in holding fast to hope for a better tomorrow, review: Chapters I, XXII, and XXIII.

11. For books you might recommend to your husband so he can better understand you and his role, see:

Ken Nair, *Discovering the Mind of a Woman,* 1982, order from Alpha Omega Publications, 404 W. 21st Street, Tempe, AZ 85282.

Weldon M. Hardenbrook, *Missing From Action,* Thomas Nelson Publishers, Nashville, TN, 1987.

And now, dear ladies, I trust my God to shower His abundant grace upon each of you who commits herself to living according to His design for biblical womanhood.

> *Now the God of hope fill you with all joy and peace in believing, that ye may abound in hope, through the power of the Holy Spirit.*
> *Romans 15:13*

> *To God, only wise, be glory through Jesus Christ forever. Amen.*　　　　*Romans 16:27*

APPENDIX

APPENDIX

WOMEN ALONE

Marriage is a God-ordained institution that is meant to provide family order for men and women while they live upon this earth. There is no marriage in heaven.

> *For in the resurrection they neither marry, nor are given in marriage, but are like the angels of God in heaven.* Matthew 22:30

Neither a woman's salvation, her ability to live the Christian way of life, nor her Christian maturity are dependent on her ever being married. Some women are called by God to remain unmarried. Paul said that singleness can be a specialized gift from God.

> *For I would that all men were even as I myself. But every man hath his proper gift of God, one after this manner, and another after that. I say, therefore, to the unmarried and widows, It is good for them if they abide as I.* I Corinthians 7:7-8

There are two categories of single women. There are the women who have never been married and those who are widowed or divorced. In either category a woman has certain responsibilities, privileges, and restrictions for living as a biblical woman. You will notice that most of the scriptural information concerning singleness has been taken from the Old Testament. This is because the Old Testament is where God recorded the laws for all human institutions.

The Woman Who Has Never Been Married

God provides for the unmarried girl through the institution of the family. He intends for a young woman to remain under the authority of her father until she marries *(Numbers 30:3-5)*. And, she should not marry without her father's permission *(I Corinthians 7:36-38)*.

* The responsibilities of an unmarried daughter include:

1. To honor and obey her parents *(Exodus 20:12; Exodus 21:15,17; Deuteronomy 5:16; 27:16; and Ephesians 6:2)*.

2. To learn the Word of God *(Deuteronomy 29:18 & 29)*.

3. To not shame her father by being promiscuous *(Leviticus 21:9)*.

* Her privileges include:

1. Protection and provision under her father's leadership. *(Numbers 30:16; II Samuel 12:3; and Job 42:15)*

2. An orphaned woman may receive the leadership and provisional care of her nearest relative (brother, uncle, etc). (The book of *Ruth*; and *Esther 2:7*). God, Himself, acts as her father if there are no male relatives to guide the unmarried woman *(Psalm 68:5)*.

3. A single woman has the privilege of being less encumbered with the cares of this world than her married sister *(I Corinthians 7:28)*. An unmarried woman has more time to develop her personal relationship with Christ *(I Corinthians 7:34)*.

* Her restrictions include:

1. An unmarried daughter is restricted from making vows that do not have her father's approval. Her father's authority extends to the negation of any vows that she might make *(Numbers 30:3-5)*.

2. An unmarried woman is to remain chaste *(Deuteronomy 22:21; I Thessalonians 4:3-5)*.

The Widow and the Divorced Woman

In today's world we have many women who are either widowed or divorced. A woman in either of these conditions also has responsibilities, privileges, and restrictions. First, she is personally responsible to God for any vows that she makes *(Numbers 30:9)*.

*   Her privileges include:

1.   A right to receive care from her relatives *(Leviticus 22:13; I Timothy 5:4 & 8).*

2.   Widows may also receive care from the church *(I Timothy 5:5-9).*

3.   A previously married woman no longer has a husband to protect her, but God will act as her husband and He will be as a father to her children *(Psalms 10:14; 10:18; 68:5;* and *82:3).*

*   Her restrictions include:

1.   A Christian widow should remarry only a fellow believer *(I Corinthians 7:39; II Corinthians 6:14).*

2.   A divorcee is restricted from remarriage for at least as long as her former husband is alive and reconciliation remains a viable possibility. *(Matthew 5:32-33; Mark 10:11-12; I Corinthians 7:10-11; 7:13-16;* and *7:27).*

Advice to the Unmarried Woman

The material in this book is directed primarily to the married woman, however, if you are single you can still benefit by reading it in its entirety. This book contains information that will help you in the following areas:

1. Being aware that your design and purpose is very different from a man's.

2. Becoming more knowledgeable concerning your responsibilities, should you marry in the future.

3. Understanding what it means to remain a single woman. A woman does not leave her femininity at the door just because she is not married. For instance, you will not have to follow the leadership of a husband, but a better understanding of God's design for womanhood and manhood will help you treat all men with the proper respect and appreciation, and in return to solicit the proper respect for yourself. Understanding God's design for womanhood will also help you choose an appropriate occupation or ministry. Furthermore, a knowledge of biblical womanhood may help you to avoid those who would corrupt your mind, body, and spirit.

4. Considering the biblical eligibility of any man who wishes to court you. (The only reason for a man and woman to spend time together alone is to determine if they should marry.) As a single woman you have

more choice than your married sister who reads this book **after** she is already married. You have the opportunity of gaining some very valuable information before you make any marriage commitment.

Do not consider giving up your single life until you have read this entire book. After which, you will be better prepared to answer the following questions before you say "I do."

1. Am I committed to honoring God's design for womanhood?

2. Do I know the intended man's family well? Do his father **and** mother treat each other in a biblical manner and are their standards compatible with my own?

3. Does my father approve of this man and his family? (If no father exists, an elder brother or a church elder could be consulted.)

4. Is the man committed to God's will for his life?

5. Does he consider his biblical responsibilities in marriage to be important?

6. Does he desire to provide for a family or does he want a financial partnership?

7. Does he take his responsibility as the spiritual leader of a family seriously?

8. Are his standards and way of life compatible with my own?

9. Do I want to change something about him? (Watch out! Whatever you presently see is what you get—it may never change and is even likely to get worse.)

10. Is he considerate, tender, and protective toward me in the way he speaks and acts towards me? Does he consider my safety before he takes me anywhere?

11. Does he exhibit clear leadership that I can follow?

12. Does he desire to lead a wife or does he appear to want a mother to serve and lead him?

13. Am I willing to love, respect, and submit to him in a biblical manner? Am I ready to trust this man with my body, mind, and emotions?

As a woman approaches her thirties or forties she sometimes feels panicky if she is still unwed. However, you are much better off remaining unwed until (or unless) God brings a man into your life who fits His design for biblical manhood. The key to happiness in life (married or single) is to be content in whatever state that you find yourself.

> *. . . for I have learned, in whatever state I am, in this to be content.*   *Philippians 4:11*

May God reveal His plan for your life. May He bless and lead you as a faithful husband.

NOTES

1. *The Unique Creation of Mankind*, (The Foundation for Biblical Research, Austin Texas, 1981). A theological study.

2. Jess Stein, ed., *The Random House College Dictionary*, (rev. ed.; NY: Random House, 1975), p. 615, s.v. "helper" and it's synomyms.

3. John Piper and Wayne Grudem, eds., *Recovering Biblical Manhood and Womanhood*, (Wheaton, Illinois: Crossway Books, a division of Good News Publishers, 1991), pp. 108, 109.

4. *The Compact Edition of the Oxford English Dictionary*, (Oxford: Oxford University Press, 1971), p.143, s.v. "authority."

5. J. Richard Fugate, *What the Bible Says About . . . Child Training*, (Tempe, Arizona: Aletheia Division of Alpha Omega Publications, 1980), p. 22. Hebrew, *'elyon*, "high, supreme' from the verb *'alah*, "go up, ascend."

6. Ibid., p. 24. Greek, *exousia* "authority"; those who are in a position of authority "officials, governments" (Romans 13:2; Luke 12:11; Titus 3:1).

7. Ibid., Greek, *tasso* "arrange, put in a place"; here

referring to the authorities "instituted" (or arranged) by God.

8. *Obedience,* (The Foundation for Biblical Research, Austin Texas, 1981). A theological study of God's institutions.

9. Ibid., Submission.

10. For a more in depth study of the woman's natural tendencies, read *Gender Sanity,* edited by Nicolas Davidson, (Lanham, MD: University Press of America,1989).

11. Jess Stein, ed,. *The Random House College Dictionary,* (rev. ed.; NY: Random House, 1975), p. 422, s.v. "ego".

12. *Arizona Republic,* January 27, 1990, p. C-2.

13. Paul Kurtz, "Fulfilling Feminist Ideals: A New Agenda," *Free Inquiry,* Fall 1990, p.21, as cited in *Understanding the Times,* David A. Noebel, (Manitou Springs, CO: Summit Press, 1991), p. 436.

14. Julian Huxley, *The Best of Humanism,* ed. Roger E. Greeley, 1945, (Buffalo: Prometheus, 1988), as cited in *Understanding the Times,* p. 116.

15. Elizabeth Cady Stanton, *Eighty Years and More,* 1898, as cited in *The Harper Book of American Quotations,* Gorton Carruth & Eugene Ehrich, (N.Y., Harper & Row, Publishers, Inc., 1988), p. 495.

16. Annie Laurie Gaylor, "Feminist 'Salvation,'" *The*

Humanist, July/August, 1988, p. 37, as cited in *Understanding the Times*, p. 486.

17. Gloria Steinem, *Outrageous Acts And Everyday Rebellions*, (Hinsdale, IL: Holt, Rinehart and Winston, 1983), p. 283.

18. Gloria Steinem, as cited in *Peter's Quotations: Ideas For Our Time*, Dr. Lawrence J. Peter, (New York: Bantam Books, 1977), as cited in *Never Too Early*, Doreen Claggett, (Melbourne, Florida, Dove Christian Books, 1989), p. 142.

19. Sol Gordon, "The Egalitarian Family is Alive and Well," *The Humanist*, May/June, 1975, p. 18, as cited in *Understanding the Times*, p. 436.

20. Dr. Joyce Brothers, "Why Wives Have Affairs," *Arizona Republic*, February, 19, 1990, Parade section, p. 5.

21. *Lynne Smith and Bob Sipchen* "Most Parents Would Give Up Careers, Poll Says," *Arizona Republic*, August 12, 1990, p. A-1. This survey was commissioned by the "Los Angeles Times" of 1,000 households in southern California's Los Angeles and Orange counties.

22. Barry Lester, Ph.D., professor of psychiatry and pediatrics at Brown University and Bradley Hospital in Providence, Rhode Island discusses communication between mother and child as cited by Susan Goodman, "Presumed Innocents," *Modern Maturity* magazine, 1992, December/January, p. 27.